CAMROSE LUTHERAN COLLEGE
CAMROSE, ALBERTA

The Gold Bug

and Other Stories

D0503323

THE GOLD BUG

and Other Stories

by

Edgar Allan Poe

As Adapted by
WILLIAM KOTTMEYER
Director, Reading Clinic
St. Louis Public Schools

Illustrated by
P. W. Shoyer

WEBSTER PUBLISHING COMPANY
St. Louis   Dallas   Atlanta   Los Angeles

CAMROSE LUTHERAN COLLEGE
LIBRARY

THE EVERYREADER LIBRARY

THE GOLDBUG AND OTHER STORIES

SIMON BOLIVAR

IVANHOE

A TALE OF TWO CITIES

CASES OF SHERLOCK HOLMES

Other Titles in Preparation

PS
2615
A1 /694

Copyright, according to the *Acts of Congress,* in the year 1947. Copyrights have also been obtained in *Great Britain* and the *British Dominions* and *Possessions.*

Printed in the United States of America.

CAMROSE LUTHERAN COLLEGE
CAMROSE, ALBERTA

CONTENTS

v

THE MURDERS IN THE
RUE MORGUE

DURING the summer of 18.... I lived in Paris. There I got to know a clever young man, C. Auguste Dupin. Dupin came from a fine French family. Lately they had lost their money. Dupin himself had a little money left. He was living alone when I met him. What extra money he had he spent for books.

I liked Dupin. I had plenty of money. I was on a vacation. I wanted to see Paris. Dupin liked me. He was almost broke. He knew Paris. So we rented a big old house and moved in together.

We spent the days talking, arguing, and sleeping.

We saw Paris at night. Right after dark, we would go out. We often walked the streets until morning.

Dupin surprised me again and again. He had read so much, he knew something about everything. He saw things I never noticed. He knew a lot about famous people in Paris. He knew college professors. They often came to him for help. He knew crooks and thieves. He knew how they worked. He read all the crime news in the newspapers. Soon he got me to reading about crimes, too. We often spent hours arguing about the police cases. Several times the Paris Police did not solve cases quickly. Then Dupin would read all the papers. Three or four times he had the answer to the cases just from the newspaper stories. About a week or two later the police would prove Dupin had been right.

"Dupin," I often said, "you should be a detective. You like to solve puzzles. You're good at it. You've got a lot of time. "Oh," he'd say, "some day I will--maybe."

One evening we sat reading the Paris papers. As usual, I looked for the crime news. "Look, Dupin," I cried. "Here is something for you."

"What is it?"

"A terrible murder—two murders."

"Read it."

I began to read:

2

" 'At three o'clock this morning Madame Lespan and her daughter Camille were brutally murdered in the Rue Morgue ———' "

"Rue Morgue ———. Wait a minute," said Dupin. "Oh, yes, I know the street. Go on."

" 'Neighbors were awakened by screams from the fourth floor of the old Lespan house. The neighbors found the doors locked. A Paris policeman broke down the door with a crowbar. By this time the cries had stopped. Neighbors and police rushed up the stairs. Two angry voices could be heard somewhere above. When the people reached the second floor, all was quiet. They quickly searched all the rooms. A large back room on the fourth floor was locked. The key was inside the lock. The policeman broke the door open. Here the terrible crime had been done.

" 'Someone had broken up the furniture and thrown it around the room. The mattress lay on the floor. On a chair lay a bloody razor. An earring, three silver spoons, and some coins were on the floor. In a corner lay two bags with four thousand francs in gold. The dresser drawers stood open. Clothing had been pulled out and thrown around the room. A small iron safe stood under the bed. It was open, with the key still in the door. A few old letters lay inside the safe.

" 'A great pile of soot lay in the fireplace. The policeman examined the chimney. Here he found the daughter, Camille Lespan. The body had been pushed up the chimney. The policeman and others could hardly pull her down. Her face was badly scratched. There were dark bruises on her throat. She had been choked to death.

" 'The rest of the house was searched. At last the neighbors and policeman went into the back yard. Here they found the body of Madame Lespan. Her throat was badly cut. Her body was badly bruised.

" 'The Paris Police are working hard on the case. Chief Gerand's men have no clue yet. Chief Gerand hopes to have the murderer in a day or two.' "

Dupin smiled.

"Chief Gerand always hopes to catch his man in a day or two," he said.

"Here's a case for you, Dupin. Why don't you find the murderer for them?"

"Oh, give them a chance. Let's see what happens first."

The next day the paper had more news. The witnesses had told their stories. Again I read while Dupin sat and smoked his pipe.

Murders in the Rue Morgue

" 'Many witnesses have been called in the Rue

Morgue murders. The police still have no clue to the brutal killer of Madame Lespan and her daughter, Camille.' "

"Does the paper give the witnesses' stories?" asked Dupin.

"Yes. Here they are." I found the part Dupin wanted.

" 'Pauline Dubourg told the police: "I knew Madame Lespan and Camille for three years. I washed their clothes for them. Madame and Camille got along fine together. They paid me well. I don't know how they made their living. I think Madame Lespan told fortunes. I always thought they had plenty of money put away. I never saw anybody else in the house. They had no servants. There was furniture only on the fourth floor." ' "

"Only on the fourth floor?" asked Dupin.

"Yes. Here's another witness. He says something about that. This is a Pierre Moreau. He's a neighbor. He has a little store near the Lespan house."

I read his story:

" 'I've lived in the Rue Morgue all my life. Madame Lespan came into my store for about four years. She and Camille lived in their house about six years. Before that they rented it to a jeweler. He rented out the upper floors to other people. Madame Lespan didn't like that. So she told them

6

all to get out. Then she moved in herself. I think the old lady was childish. I saw the girl only five, or six times in all. I heard they had a lot of money. The neighbors say the old lady told fortunes. I don't think she did. I never saw anybody else go into the house except the doctor.' "

"They weren't a very friendly pair," said Dupin.

"No," I said. "They didn't meet anybody to be friendly with."

"But then, they didn't make enemies, either."

"The paper says the other neighbors saw no one visit them, either. No one even knows if they have any relatives. They kept the front window shutters closed. The back shutters were, too, except on the fourth floor."

"What does the policeman say?"

I found the story told by Isidore Muset, the policeman. I read:

" 'Someone called me about three o'clock in the morning. I ran to the Lespan house. I found about twenty people trying to get in. I pushed them aside. I asked what was the matter. They told me someone was screaming in the house. I could hear it myself, then. I broke open the door. When the door fell in, the screams stopped. I leaped up the stairs. The others followed. When I got to the first floor I could hear two voices. It sounded as if they were arguing. One voice was low and rough. The other one was a strange shrill voice. I could make out a word or two spoken by the first voice. The words were French. The voice was a man's voice. The high, shrill voice was not speaking French, though. I'm not sure whether it was a man's voice or a woman's. I couldn't make out any words, but I think it was Spanish.' "

"Well," said Dupin. "That helps a little. Any others who heard the voices?"

"Yes," I said. I kept on reading.

" 'My name is Henri Duval. I'm a neighbor. I was right in back of the policeman. He broke the door in. Some of us ran in with him. I stopped to set up the door again. The crowd was getting pretty big outside. I heard the voices, too. I think the shrill voice was an Italian. I know it wasn't French. I'm not sure if it was a man's voice, or a woman's. I can't speak Italian myself, but the voice sounded Italian to me. I knew Madame Lespan and Camille. I've talked to them often. I know the voice was not Madame Lespan's nor Camille's.' "

"They seem to be mixed up on their languages," said Dupin.

"Here's another one," I said, reading ahead. "Here's a fellow named Odenheimer. They got his story, too. But they had to translate it. He's a

Dutchman. Can't speak French. Here's his story:

"'I was passing the house. I heard the screams. They lasted about ten minutes. They were long and loud. I went in with the policeman. I'm sure the shrill voice was that of a man. I'm sure it was in French. The voice sounded afraid and angry.'"

"Anything there about the money in the room?" asked Dupin.

I read further.

"Yes," I said. "Madame Lespan's banker was called in. He said Madame Lespan owned several houses. She had kept her money in his bank for about eight years. She often brought in money. It was always in small amounts. Three days before her death she took out 4,000 francs. They gave her the money in gold. They even sent a clerk to carry it home for her."

"A bank clerk?"

"Yes. His name is Adolphe LeBon."

"LeBon—I know him," said Dupin. "What did he have to say?"

"He went home with Madame Lespan. It was about noon. He carried the 4,000 francs in two bags. When they got there Camille was at the door. She took one bag. Madame Lespan took the other. No one saw them. The street is very lonely."

"I'm interested in that high shrill voice they

heard," said Dupin. "Did any other witness hear it?"

"Yes," I said. "Here's the story told by William Bird. He's a tailor—an Englishman. He's lived in Paris for about two years. He says this:

" 'I was one of the first to go up the stairs. I heard the voices upstairs, too. The rough voice was talking French. I heard several French words clearly. There was a scraping sound. The shrill voice was very loud. I know it wasn't English or French. I'd say it was German. No, I don't know German. It just sounded German to me.' "

"Now I'm still more interested in that voice," said Dupin. "No two witnesses tell the same story."

"There's some more here about that," I said.

"First, something else. How did the killer get away? He couldn't have passed all those people."

"The fourth floor was locked on the *inside*. All the witnesses say that. Everything was quiet. When they broke that door down, they saw no one. The windows were locked on the inside. The hall door was locked on the inside. A little room was filled with old boxes. The neighbors looked carefully there. They looked into all the chimneys. Nobody could get out that way. The house is four stories high. There is a trap door to the roof. They looked at that. It was nailed down. They say it took from three to five minutes to get into the room."

"Well," said Dupin. "People just don't jump out of fourth floor windows."

"And the witnesses said the chimneys were too small to get through. There is no back door on the fourth floor."

"Well, we'll see about that. You say someone else heard the voices?"

"Yes. Alfonzo Garcio, a Spaniard. He lives in the Rue Morgue. He ran into the house after the policeman. But he didn't go upstairs. He knows the rough voice was French. The shrill voice was English, he says. He doesn't speak English himself, though!"

"Oh," said Dupin, "another one."

"There's one more. This one is an Italian, Alberto Montani. He says he was one of the first ones upstairs. He, too, says the first voice was French. He couldn't make out the words spoken by the shrill voice. He thinks it was Russian, though. But he doesn't speak Russian."

"Did the doctor say anything? The police always have the bodies examined."

"Yes, Dr. Paul Dumas examined the bodies. Nothing more than we know, though. He found finger marks on the girl's throat. The old lady was badly bruised. Dumas says a very strong man must have used a club. He says no woman could have done it."

"Does Chief Gerand still hope to catch the killer in a day or two?" Dupin smiled.

"No," I laughed. "Not today. The paper says the police haven't got a clue."

The evening papers told little new. The police had searched the house again. They had examined witnesses once more. They had arrested Adolphe LeBon, the bank clerk. I could see Dupin was interested in the case.

"What do you think of it?" he asked me.

"They'll never catch the man. It's too late. I don't know how he got away, but he's gone," I said.

"Don't be too sure. The Paris police are good in their way. They're careful. They work hard. But they don't use their brains. They go after every case the same way. They never change. Let's go take a look, ourselves. Maybe we'll find something they missed. Besides, this LeBon once did me a favor. I'd like to help him out."

"But how will we get in?"

"I know Gerand, the Police Chief. He'll let us in."

So we went to the Rue Morgue. We got there in the late afternoon. A crowd of people stood on the sidewalk, talking about the murders. We didn't go right in. We walked up the street and turned down an alley. We turned again and went in the back. Dupin led the way. He looked very carefully at everything. Then we turned around and went back to the front. A policeman stood at the front door. Dupin showed him a note from Gerand. He let us in.

We went upstairs. The police had moved nothing. The bodies of the women were still there. Everything was as the newspaper had said. Dupin examined everything. Then we went into the other rooms and the yard. All this took us until dark. Then we left. On the way Dupin stopped at a newspaper office. Then we went home.

Dupin wouldn't say a word about the case. About noon the day after, he suddenly asked:

"Did you see anything *strange* at the Lespan house?"

"No," I said. "It was just as the paper said."

"Everybody thinks this mystery is hard to solve. They think it's hard because it's so unusual. I say a mystery is easy when it's unusual."

"That's too deep for me," I said.

"Here's why the police are puzzled. They can't see why the killer was so brutal. Why were the bodies so bruised? Here's another thing they're puzzled about. Everybody hears two voices. They run upstairs. Nobody is there. And there's no way to get out. Then, why was the room messed up? Why was Camille pushed into the chimney? All this is unusual. That's why the police think it's a hard case. I say it's an easy case. It's easy because it's unusual."

I looked at Dupin in surprise.

"You don't mean—," I said. "You don't mean you've solved this mystery already?"

"I am now waiting for a man." Here Dupin looked at the door. "I am now waiting for a man who is mixed up in it. He didn't kill Madame Lespan and Camille himself. I look for this man here—in this room—any minute. He may not come. But I think he will. If he does, we may have to hold him. Here are the pistols. We both know how to use them. I hope we won't need them."

I was so surprised I could hardly hold the gun. Dupin went on talking.

"The voices the neighbors heard were not Madame Lespan's nor Camille's. So the old lady could not have killed the girl and then herself. Anyway, she wasn't strong enough. She couldn't have pushed Camille up the chimney. She couldn't have beat herself. So someone else did it. The ones whose voices were heard did it. Now let's go back to the voices. What was strange about the voices?"

"Why, everybody said the rough voice was French. But nobody agreed on the other voice."

"Yes. That's what the witnesses said. But that

wasn't the strange part. Everybody did say the rough voice was French. But the other voice! The Frenchman says it was Spanish. But the Spaniard says it was English. The Dutchman says it was French. But not one Frenchman says it was French. The Englishman thinks it was German. But he knows no German. The Spaniard says it was English. But the Englishman knows it wasn't. The Italian says it was Russian. But he has never heard Russian. The second Frenchman says the voice was Italian. But the Italian thinks it was Russian. Here we have French, English, Spanish, Italian, and Dutch people. Not one hears his *own* language. All think it's another langauge. So it was none of these."

"Couldn't it have been a language of Asia or Africa?"

"Well, I'm sure it wasn't. There aren't many people from Asia or Africa in Paris. And no one heard one word. They heard a voice but not one word.

"Well, what does that mean?"

"I'll tell you later what that means. Let's go back to something else. How did the murderers get out? Let's take every way they could get out. They were in the room where Camille was found or next door. They had to get out of those two rooms. The police examined the ceilings and walls.

I examined them myself. There are no secret doors. Both doors were locked with the keys inside. How about the chimneys? They get narrower the higher they go. A cat can't get through. The trap door was nailed shut. That leaves only the windows. They didn't get out the front windows. The crowd in the street would have seen them. So they *must* have got out the back windows."

"How could they?" I asked. "They're on the fourth floor."

"There are two windows. One has a bed in front of it. The other one is clear. The police tried this window. It was fastened *inside*. They couldn't raise it. There was a hole in the window frame. A thick nail was stuck in the hole to keep the window down. The other window was fixed the same way. The police couldn't raise this window either. So they gave up on the windows."

"I don't blame them. I'd have given up, too."

"But the window was the *only* way to get out. There was no other way. The killers couldn't get out the window *and* fasten the window from inside. But the windows were fastened. What's the answer?"

"You tell me, Dupin."

"They must fasten by themselves."

"Now, Dupin listen—"

"It had to be. I stepped to the window. I pulled

out the nail. I tried to raise the window. It wouldn't open. I knew it wouldn't. There had to be a hidden spring. I looked carefully. I found it. I pressed it. Now I could raise the window."

"But how could they put the nail back in? How could they from the outside?"

"They couldn't. So I knew they hadn't used that window. They must have got out the other window. I pulled the bed aside. I looked at the window carefully. I found the same kind of nail. I took hold of it. About half of it came out. The other half stayed. I stuck it back. It looked like an unbroken nail. I found the spring. I pressed it. The window went up. The half nail went up with it. I closed the window. Again it looked as if the window were nailed shut."

"I see. The killer got out that window. He closed it. The police thought it was nailed shut. They tried to open it. They couldn't. They thought the nail held the window shut. But it was really the spring."

"That's right," said Dupin. "Now, how did he get down? Remember we walked to the back of the building? About five and a half feet from the window is a lightning rod."

"But how could he get to the lightning rod?"

"Did you see the shutter on that window?"

"No."

"There's just one big shutter. It's like a door. It's about three and a half feet wide. The shutter was standing straight out when we looked. But if you swing the shutter back to the wall, it's only two feet from the lightning rod. You could climb up the lightning rod to the fourth floor. You could grab hold of the shutter. You could push with your feet against the wall. You could swing yourself to the window. If the window were open you could jump right into the room."

"I couldn't do it."

"No, and I couldn't either. Very few men could. It's dangerous and hard to do. Think of this. Here's something few men can do. Now think of the shrill voice again. Nobody knew the language it spoke. All heard a voice but heard no words."

A cold chill began to creep over me. I shivered!

"Dupin, you don't mean—"

"I said somebody could get in that way. So somebody could get out that way, too. I mean it. The killer got out that way. But he got in that way, too. He didn't come up the stairs at all. And about robbing the place. No one took anything. The stuff was thrown all over the room. But the four thousand francs were still there. No, nothing was stolen."

"That makes sense to me," I said.

"Now, about the murders. Camille was pushed

up the chimney. They could hardly get her down. Whoever pushed her up there was very, very powerful. And there was no sense to it. The body would surely be found. The doctors said Madame Lespan was badly bruised. They thought someone had hit her with a club. She wasn't bruised by a club. Someone threw her from the window."

"Threw her from the window?"

"Yes. The police didn't think of that. They thought the windows had not been opened. Now, we have a room torn up. No sense to it. We have a killer who is a wonderful climber. The killer is very powerful. He is brutal. He has no reason to kill. He makes sounds no one can understand. Now, what's the answer?"

"A madman," I said. "A powerful crazy man."

"Well," said Dupin, "that's a good guess. But even madmen speak a language. And madmen don't have hair like this. I found it in Madame Lespan's fist."

Here Dupin held out some bristles of hair.

"Dupin!" I cried. "This is not *human* hair!"

"I never said it was. The marks on Camille's throat were finger marks. I measured them. Then I drew them on this piece of paper. See if you can fit your fingers to the marks."

I tried to. I couldn't do it.

"This is no human hand," I said.

"I've been doing a lot of reading lately," said Dupin. "And I've got the answer. This crime wasn't human. An animal must have done it. What animal is a great climber, very strong, brutal? What animal has fingers? What animal could use a knife? What animal could push the window down? What animal can make a noise like a human voice? What animal has hair like this? What animal —"

"An ape!" I cried. " But how could —"

"Right," said Dupin. "If you will read about them you'll find the orang-outang ape can do all this. That's the murderer of the Rue Morgue!"

"But the other voice," I cried. "The French voice?"

"A Frenchman knows about the murder. He did nothing himself. But he saw what happened. The ape may have been his. He couldn't have caught it. The people were coming up the stairs. He had to get down the lightning rod and away. Remember I stopped at a newspaper office yesterday?"

"Yes."

"Well, I put an ad in today's paper. It's a paper that has news of boats and sailors. Here's my ad."

Dupin handed me a newspaper. He pointed to his ad.

"Found—In a park. Early this morning. A very large brown orang-outang ape. The sailor who lost

him may have him back. Call at No. —, Rue —
this evening after five."

Dupin had put our address in.

"How do you know he's a sailor," I asked.

"I don't know it. But at the bottom of the lightning rod I found this little ribbon. It's the kind
French sailors wear on their caps. And a sailor is
a good climber. He has to be to climb the masts.
And who would have a chance to catch an ape? A
sailor, of course."

"But why should he want the ape back? Won't
he be afraid?"

"Well, he brought the ape to Paris. Why? To
sell it, of course. He can get a lot of money from
the zoo or a circus for his ape. He can't be rich.
He saw the ape get away. How would anybody
guess an ape had done the crime? No, I think he'll
come. He'll try to get his ape back."

Just then we heard a step on the stairs.

"Be ready," said Dupin. "Hide the guns."

Someone knocked at the door.

"Come in," said Dupin.

A man came in. He was a sailor. He was tall
and strong. He looked us over carefully. He was
nervous.

"Good evening," he said.

"Sit down, my friend," said Dupin. "I guess

you've come for the ape. He's a fine animal. How old is he?"

The sailor took a deep breath. He had been worried. Now he smiled.

"I don't know. Four or five years old, I guess. Have you got him here?"

"Oh, no. I've got him at a stable down the street. You can get him in the morning. You can prove he's yours?"

"Yes, sir, I can. And I'll be glad to pay you a reward."

"A reward? Well, let me see. I know! Here's what I'll take as a reward. Just tell me everything you know about the murders in the Rue Morgue."

Dupin said this very quietly. As he did he quietly stood up and locked the door. He put the key into his pocket. He calmly took out his pistol and laid it on the table.

The sailor jumped up. He started to pick up a chair. When he saw the gun he sat down again.

"My friend," said Dupin kindly, "don't worry. We're not going to harm you. I know you did nothing wrong. You didn't even steal anything. And you could have. Couldn't you? But you must tell what you know. A man is in jail now—a man who did no crime."

"Yes," said the sailor. "I'll tell you all I know. I did nothing wrong. My ship was going to India. We stopped at Borneo. We had some time to spare. A friend and I caught the ape. We were going to bring him back and sell him. We had a lot of trouble with him. He was wild and fierce. We had to beat him often. At last I got him home. I hid him in my house. On the night of the murder I had gone out to a party. When I got back the ape was loose. I found him in my bedroom. You know how apes try to do what they see others do. He had often watched me shave. Well, there he sat, before a mirror. He had smeared soap all over his face. He had my razor in his hand, trying to shave. I didn't know what to do. I used to quiet him with a whip. I got out the whip. When he saw it he ran. Down the stairs he went. He jumped out of a window, still carrying the razor.

"I followed him. He'd wait until I got close. Then he'd run again. The streets were quiet. It was about three o'clock in the morning. I chased him a long time. At last he turned down an alley back of the Rue Morgue. He saw a light in this Madame Lespan's house. He ran into the yard. Then he saw the lightning rod. He climbed up in a minute. He grabbed the shutter and swung. He jumped into the room and slammed the shutter back. I thought

I had him trapped. But I was afraid he'd hurt some-body. So I went up the rod after him. I couldn't swing on the shutter the way he did. But I could lean over and look into the room. I did. I nearly fell when I looked. The women had started to scream. The ape had grabbed Madame Lespan and was trying to shave her. The girl had fainted. When the woman screamed the ape got angry. He swung the razor at her. She fell to the floor. Now he leaped at the girl and choked her. I yelled at him. He saw my face looking in. He remembered the whip. He got scared. He began to chatter. So he ran around, tearing up the room. I kept calling him. Then he tried to hide what he'd done. He pushed the girl into the chimney. He picked the woman up and threw her out the window. When I saw that I slid down the lightning rod and ran home."

Well, that's about all. The ape must have got out just before the policeman broke in. He must have closed the window. The sailor later caught the ape and sold it. Dupin and I went to see Gerand. Dupin told him the whole story. LeBon was turned loose right away.

That evening I looked eagerly at the newspaper. I found the crime news. There was a big headline:
RUE MORGUE MYSTERY SOLVED

"Dupin," I cried. "You are a hero. Listen, I'll read it to you."

I started to read:

" 'Chief Gerand of the Paris Police has done it again. He has solved the case of the Murders in the Rue Morgue ——.' Say, what is this?" I looked at Dupin. He was laughing quietly.

"You may think it's funny," I said hotly. "But I don't. Why, the big, fat liar! To say *he* solved the case!"

"Oh!" laughed Dupin. "Forget about it. I knew he'd do that. Some day, maybe, we'll pay him back. Who wants to be famous, anyway? Let's go out and see some more of Paris."

THE STOLEN LETTER

IT was just after dark. I was in Paris that autumn in 18—. My friend C. Auguste Dupin and I were sitting in his little book room. We had lit our pipes. Neither of us spoke. We blew great clouds of smoke and watched them float away.

We had been talking all afternoon. Dupin had answered a lot of my questions. He had become even more famous since his last detective case. The Paris newspapers were full of it. The murders of the Rue Morgue had everybody talking. Dupin had found the killer of Madame Lespan and her daughter. We had been talking about the case.

Suddenly the door flew open. Dupin and I looked up in surprise. There stood Monsieur Gerand, Chief of the Paris Police. We both had known the Chief some time. Dupin had helped him with several famous cases. The Chief liked to get help from Dupin. Dupin did the work and the Chief took the honor.

But we were glad to see him. He wasn't a very smart man. Dupin didn't think much of him as a detective. But he always had a story to tell. Sometimes he was really funny.

We had been sitting in the dark. Dupin got up to turn on the light.

"I've got a case to tell you about," said Gerand. Dupin sat down again.

"If you want me to think, let's sit in the dark," he said.

"Now, that's another one of your funny ideas," said Gerand.

Whenever the Chief didn't understand something, he called it funny. A lot of things were funny to the Chief. Dupin got him a cigar. He pushed a chair over for him. Gerand sat down and lit the cigar.

"What's the matter now?" I asked. "No more murders, I hope."

"Oh, no. Nothing like that. The case is really

an easy one. I'm sure we can work it out ourselves. I thought Dupin would like to hear about it. It's such a funny case."

"Simple and funny," said Dupin.

"Why, yes. No, wait a minute. It's simple. But we have been puzzled. We've been having some trouble. But it is simple."

"Maybe it's too simple for you," said Dupin.

"Oh, come, come, Dupin. Who ever heard of such an idea?"

"Maybe the mystery is too plain," said Dupin.

"Ha!" the Chief laughed. "That's a good one."

"A little too plain," said Dupin again.

"Ha! Ha!" laughed the Chief. "You will have your little joke."

"Well, what is this case all about?" I asked.

"Why, I'll tell you," said Gerand. He stopped laughing. He took a deep puff of his cigar. "I'll tell you in a few words. But first I must warn you. This case is a secret. No one must know about it. If it is found out, I'll lose my job."

"Go on," I said.

"Or don't tell us," said Dupin.

"Well, here it is. A letter has been stolen. It's been stolen from the King's palace. We know who stole it. There is no question about it. He was seen taking it. We know he still has it."

"How do you know he has?" Dupin asked him.

"He must have it. Something terrible will happen when he uses it. Nothing has happened. So we know he still has it."

"Can't you tell us more plainly? What's this all about?" I asked.

"Well, I can say this. The letter gives this man great power. It gives him power over someone in the King's family."

"I still don't get it," said Dupin. "You'll have to explain."

"No? Well, if a certain important man got this letter, a certain important woman would be in trouble. The man who has the letter can give it to the Ki—uh. I mean he can give it to this certain important man. And he will. He will if she doesn't do what he tells her to."

"Oh, don't try to talk like that," I said. "You mean the woman is the Queen. Why don't you say so? That is what I don't get. She has to know this man has her letter. What man dares to blackmail the Queen?"

The Chief was beginning to sweat a little.

"The man who stole the letter is Jacques Divoll. You know him. Or you've heard of him. One of the highest men in the French Government. He has an iron nerve. He's as cool as ice. He's afraid

of no one. And he stops at nothing. Brains and nerve."

"How did he get the letter?"

"Here's how it happened. The Queen gets the letter from a man she once loved. Once she had almost married him. She's alone. She reads the letter. In walks the King. She doesn't want the King to see the letter. He might not understand. He might think she writes to him. She tries to slip it in a drawer. The drawer won't open. So she lays it on a table. The side with the address is on top. The King doesn't see it, though. Now, in comes Jacques Divoll. He spots the letter. He knows the handwriting. He sees how nervous the Queen is. He guesses everything. But he's smart. He talks with the King. After a while he pulls a letter from his pocket. He reads some of it to the King. He lays it on the table next to the Queen's letter. Now he keeps on talking for about fifteen minutes. Then he gets ready to leave. He goes to the table while he's talking. He picks up the Queen's letter and leaves *his* letter there. The Queen sees him. But what can she do? The King is there. She doesn't want him to see the letter. So she says nothing. And so Divoll walks out. He's got her letter. He leaves his own."

"Ah," said Dupin to me. "She knows he's got it

all right. And he knows that she knows. He's got her just where he wants her."

"Yes," said the Chief. "He has. When he wants the King to do something, he goes to the Queen. He tells her she has to help him—or else. So she tries to get the King to do what Divoll wants. Divoll wants more and more from the King. The Queen has got to get that letter back. What can she do? At last she sends for me. I come. I promise not to tell anyone about it. I've got to get her letter for her."

"Well," said Dupin. "You're the Chief of the Paris Police. She couldn't have got a better man.". I knew Dupin was smiling.

"It's very nice of you to say so," said Gerand. He couldn't see the smile. "She thinks so, too, I guess."

"I guess you're right," I said. "Jacques Divoll must have the letter. He's got her as long as he has the letter. The only way she can end it is to tell the King all about it."

"Oh, no!" said Gerand. "She can't do that. At least, she won't. The King is very jealous. And he's pretty hot headed. No, she will never dare do that."

"What have you done to get the letter?" asked Dupin.

"The first thing I did was search Divoll's little hotel. I had to search the house while he was gone.

You see, we can't let him know what we're doing."

"I don't see why you haven't found it. The Paris police are famous for that work," I said.

"Oh, yes. That's why I wasn't worried about the case. And Divoll made it easy for us. He is often away all night. He hasn't got many servants. They don't sleep at the hotel. We can get them drunk when we need to. You know about my keys. I can open any lock in Paris. I've worked every night for three months. I myself have been there every night. We searched and searched. But we can't find it."

"I can't believe it!" I said.

"I tell you I must find it. And I'll tell you another secret. The reward is very big. I didn't quit looking until now. Jacques Divoll must be smarter than I. I have looked everywhere."

"I know you fellows are good at that. Do you think he has the letter somewhere else? He might have hidden it in some other place."

"I don't think so. He's got to be able to grab that letter any minute. He's smart enough to know that."

"Why does he? Why does he need to have it quickly?"

"He's got to be able to burn it. He's pretty sure the Queen will never tell the King about the letter. He knows her. And he knows the King. But what if somebody would find out about the letter? And what if he tipped the King off? The King would get that letter in a hurry. And what would happen to Jacques Divoll? No, he's got to have it close by. If something goes wrong, he burns it. Then nobody can prove anything."

"I see. You're right. The letter must be near. I guess he wouldn't carry it with him."

"No. I thought of that. He's been robbed twice, at night, on the street. He was carefully searched. The men who robbed him were Paris policemen. I was with them. He doesn't know that, though."

"You could have saved yourself the trouble," said Dupin. "Jacques Divoll is no fool. I know him well. He once played me a dirty trick. But he's clever—very clever. He knew you would do that. I'll bet you didn't surprise him."

"Tell us about your search," I said. "I know that letter is there somewhere."

"Well, we took our time. We looked everywhere. I've searched a lot of places. And believe me, I know how to do it. We searched the whole building. We took one room at a time. We put in a whole week on each room. First we took the furniture. We opened every drawer. We looked at everything in every drawer."

"How about secret drawers? Could there be any secret drawers?"

"For me there is no secret drawer. No good police-man misses a secret drawer. You just can't get away with it. Look. You measure the drawers. You measure the furniture. When you get extra space, you look for it. It may be behind the drawer. It may be on the sides. It may be between drawers. If it's not there, you find another drawer. We've got good tools. We measure carefully. No, I could have found any secret drawer."

"What else did you do?"

"Next we took the chairs. First we looked at the seats. Many are padded. We have long thin needles for that. You've seen me use them. We push them into the seats. You can't tell we've used them. But if anything is hidden there, we find it. We looked at every chair in the building. Next we took the table tops off."

"Why did you do that?"

"Well, look. This is what people sometimes do. They first take off the table top. Then they bore a hole in the leg. That makes a good hiding place. They put the top back on. You'd never guess any-thing was there. We looked at the bottoms and tops of all the bedposts, too. You can do the same thing with them."

"Couldn't you just tap them? If they were hollow you'd hear it, wouldn't you?" I asked.

"No. They can fool you. You put the thing you're hiding in the hole. Then you stuff the hole with cotton. Tap all you want. The wood sounds solid. Anyway, we had to be careful. We couldn't make any noise."

"But you couldn't take everything apart. He could roll that letter very thin. He could have slipped it almost anywhere. Couldn't he put it in a chair leg? Or in one of the chair rungs? Don't tell me you took all the chairs apart."

"No, we didn't. But we did better than that. We looked carefully at every chair rung in the hotel. We have strong microscopes for that. If he had taken a rung out, we would have known it. The microscopes will show a single grain of sawdust. The rungs are glued in. If you take a rung out, you crack the glue. The microscopes would show that, too. No, he couldn't get away with it."

"Did you look at the mirrors? Or behind the woodwork? How about the beds? And the sheets and pillows? Did you go over the curtains? Did you look at the rugs?"

"Every one. Everything. We took every stick of furniture in the place. Then we looked over the building itself. We examined every inch with the microscopes. We even took the two houses next door. We went over them just as carefully."

"Two other houses!" I said. "You really did a good job. You went to a lot of trouble."

"Yes, we did. But the reward is very big. I'd do a lot more to get that reward."

"Did you look in the grounds around the house?"

"The ground is all paved with brick. That gave us little trouble. We took our microscopes again. We looked at every crack between the bricks. No one had moved a brick."

"Did you look through Divoll's papers? How about the books in his library?"

"Yes, we took care of those things, too. We opened every package and every box. We read all the papers. We opened every book. We turned over every page in every book. We measured every book cover. We looked at every cover with microscopes. We would have found anything hidden there. Divoll had just had new covers put on five or six books. We went over them very carefully. We used the needles on them, too."

"You looked at the floors under the rugs?"

"Yes. We took up every rug. We examined the rugs. Then we looked at the floors with microscopes."

"And the paper on the walls?"

"Yes."

"You looked into the cellars?"

"We did."

"Then you must be wrong," I said. "The letter is not there. It can't be."

"I'm afraid you're right," said Gerand. "And now, Dupin. What would you advise me to do?"

"Look everything through again."

"But why? I know it's not there. We were most careful. We can't do the job better."

"I can't give you any better advice. You know what the letter looks like, don't you?"

"Oh, yes." The Chief took out his notebook. He read to us how the letter looked. We talked a while longer. Then the Chief left. He was not feeling very cheerful.

About a month later he came back to us. We were sitting in the same room. Dupin gave him a cigar again. He pulled up the chair for him. We talked a while. Then I said,

"Well, Gerand, how about the stolen letter? Have you given up?"

"I'm afraid Jacques Divoll has me beat. I went over the hotel again, as Dupin here advised. Did the whole job all over. But we didn't find the letter. Well, I knew we wouldn't."

"By the way, Gerand," said Dupin. "The reward. How much did you say it was?"

"Why, a great deal. It's a very good reward. It's been doubled since I saw you. I don't want to tell just how much. But I will say this. I'll give anybody my check for fifty thousand francs for that letter. We need the letter more than ever. I can't do any more than I have to get it."

"Oh, I wouldn't say that," said Dupin. He puffed on his pipe for a minute. "You could do a little more. Yes, I think so."

"But how? In what way?"

"Why, you could hire a detective."

"Hire a detective? I'm a detective. Why should I hire a detective?"

"You could hire the right one. You've heard the story they tell about Dr. Abernethy?"

"No. What has Dr. Abernethy got to do with this?"

"Why, a rich miser tried to get free help from the Doctor. This miser needed a doctor. One day he was talking to Doctor Abernethy. So he told him just how he felt. But he told Dr. Abernethy he was talking about another man. Dr. Abernethy caught on right away. Then the miser said, 'What would you have told him to take, Doctor?' 'Why,' said Abernethy, 'he should take a doctor's advice.'"

"But I'm willing to take advice," said the Chief. "And I'm willing to pay for it. I really would give fifty thousand francs to the man who helps me. I would write a check this minute."

"Well," said Dupin. "If that's the way you feel about it."

He opened a drawer in his desk.

"Here's a check book. You may write me a check for fifty thousand francs. When you put your name on it I'll give you the letter."

My mouth opened in surprise. I looked at Dupin. Could he be joking? He didn't smile. The Chief's eyes were popping. For a minute or two he didn't move. He too just looked at Dupin. He couldn't believe it. Then he grabbed a pen. He looked at Dupin again. At last he wrote the check for fifty thousand francs. He put his name on it. Then he handed it to Dupin. Dupin looked at it. He folded it and calmly put it in his pocket. He walked over to his desk. He unlocked a drawer. He picked up a letter and carelessly threw it to the Chief. The Chief almost fell out of his chair. He grabbed for it. His hands were shaking. At last he got it open. He read the letter. The sweat stood out on his head. Suddenly he leaped to his feet. He rushed to the door. On the way he fell over a chair. He scrambled to his feet again. He ran. The door slammed.

* * * *

Dupin laughed as the Chief ran out.

"All right," I said. "You clever rascal. Tell me how you got it."

We lit our pipes again and sat down. Dupin started.

"The Paris Police are good. They're very good. They stick to a job. They're fairly smart. Sometimes they're clever. They know a lot about crooks. The Chief told us how they had searched that hotel. I knew they had done a good job. As far as they went, they were very good."

"What do you mean? 'As far as they went'?"

"If Jacques Divoll had hidden the letter where they looked, they would have found it. He could not have kept it from them."

"Well, why didn't they find it then?"

"I say they did a good job. But they work on all cases the same way. They never change. If a stupid man hides something, they look as they did. If a smart man hides something, they look in the same places. The Chief doesn't use his head. I know some school boys who can think better than he."

"Oh, come, Dupin. Not a school boy!"

"Yes, a school boy. I knew one about eight or nine years old. The boys played a game at school. They used marbles. The game is called 'odd and even.' This is how you play it. One boy holds some marbles in his closed hand. He asks the other boy whether the number of marbles is odd or even. If the boy guesses right, he wins a marble. If he guesses wrong, the other boy wins one. My young friend won all the marbles in the school."

"How did he do it?"

"He tried to figure out how smart the other boy was. Here's the way he did it. Suppose he plays with a stupid boy. The stupid boy holds up his hand and asks, 'Odd or even?' My little friend says odd. Let's say he loses. Then he tries it again. My friend thinks this way: This boy is stupid. The first time he had an even number of marbles. He's got just enough sense to change this time to odd. I'll guess 'odd' again. He does. He wins. He keeps on winning."

"But all the boys aren't that stupid."

"No. When he plays with a smarter boy he figures it out this way. This boy held an even number of marbles. I guessed 'odd.' The first thing he'll want to do is change the number to odd. That's what the stupid boy did. But this fellow is smarter. He'll keep the number even to fool me. I'll guess 'even.' He guesses 'even.' He wins again. He wins often. The other boys say he's lucky. He isn't lucky at all. He uses his head. Do you see what I mean?"

"Yes, I guess so. He just figures out how smart the other fellow is. When he knows that he can guess what he'll do."

"That's it," said Dupin. "I was interested in that boy. I talked to him. I said, 'How can you always figure out how smart the other boys are? How can you tell what they're thinking'?"

"He said, 'Sometimes I want to know how smart a boy is. Sometimes I want to know how good or bad he is. Sometimes I want to know what he is thinking about. So I watch his face. I try to look the same way. If he smiles, I smile the same way. If he moves his eyes, I move mine. If he turns his face away, I turn mine. Then thoughts come to my mind. If I make my face like his, I think the same way he does. That's the way I tell what he's thinking.' "

"But does that work?"

"Yes, often it does. A lot of smart men do the same thing. That's how they know what the other fellow will do. Other people think they're very wise. It's really simple."

"Well, you do have to figure out how smart the other fellow is."

"Yes, that's right," said Dupin. "That's why the Chief gets fooled. He never tries to figure the other fellow out. He thinks only what he himself would do. Jacques Divoll hides the letter. The Chief tries to find it. He doesn't look where Divoll would hide it. He looks where he himself would hide it."

"But he gets some of the men he's after."

"Yes, he does. He gets them when they are about as smart as he is. But when they're smarter, he doesn't. And when they are more stupid, he doesn't. Now look at this case of the stolen letter. The Chief figures out where he himself would hide it. He knows he would hide it in some secret place. So he thinks every one else would, too. He looks only in secret places."

"Well, I think I'd do the same."

"And most of the time you'd find it. But Jacques Divoll has brains. Divoll does what my little school boy did. He figures out how smart the Chief is. He figures out where the Chief will look. He knows the Chief will do just what he did do. So he doesn't hide the letter there."

"What does he do?"

"I'm coming to that. He makes it too easy for the Chief."

"Too easy?"

"Yes. He puts the letter right under the Chief's nose."

"But how can the Chief miss it?"

"Because he doesn't look there. Have you ever looked at street signs?"

"Street signs? I guess so. Yes, I have."

"Which signs do you see quickly?"

"Why, I don't know. I never tried to remember."

"Well, here's the same idea. Boys in school play another game. This one is with maps. One boy finds a name on the map. He tells the other boy the name. It may be a town or a river. It may be a state or a country. The other boy tries to find it on the map. A boy will first try to find a tiny name in small letters. But he soon sees the other boy find it. The boys soon learn how to make the game hard. They pick names with big letters. They pick names that stretch over the page. Those are the words which are hard to see. The same idea works with street signs. The signs you see best are small ones. The big long ones are hard to see. But the Chief doesn't think of this. He didn't think Jacques Divoll would put the letter right in front of him. But that was the best way to fool him. And that's what he did."

"I see. Go on."

"Well, I knew Divoll was smart. I knew he had to have the letter near. So I figured he'd put it in the open."

"What did you do?"

"I got a pair of dark glasses. I went to visit Divoll. He knows me, so he wasn't surprised. He was just sitting around. We talked a while. I told him I was having eye trouble. Behind the glasses my eyes went over the room.

"He had a big writing table there. There were some papers and letters lying there. A few books were thrown on top. I looked at the table carefully. But I saw nothing I was looking for.

"I kept looking around the room. At last I saw a cardboard letter holder. It hung from the wall on a dirty blue ribbon. The holder had three or four pockets. I could see some cards and one letter. The letter was very dirty and wrinkled. It was torn nearly in half. It looked as if someone was going to tear it up and throw it away. I could read the address. It was written to Jacques Divoll. It had his name and hotel address on it. The name had been written by a woman. The letters were small and neatly written. The letter was carelessly stuck in the holder.

"When I saw that letter, I knew it was the one I wanted. It looked different. You'd think the Queen's letter would be carefully kept. This one was torn and dirty. The writing on the Queen's letter was by a man. This one was by a woman. The letters were a little *too* different.

"Well, I stayed a long time. We talked about guns. Jacques Divoll knows a lot about them. He has a fine collection. While we talked I looked at the letter. I wanted to remember exactly how it looked. I wanted to see how it lay in the holder. Then I saw something else. The edges of the letter were wrinkled and rough. I guessed what Divoll had done. He had simply turned the Queen's letter inside out. Then he had somebody write his name and address on it. When I saw that I left. I said good-bye to Divoll. But I was careful to leave my pipe and tobacco on the table.

"The next morning I went back. I asked Divoll if I had left my pipe. We found it. We started talking about guns again. Suddenly we heard a loud bang. It sounded like a gun shot. People outside began to scream. Divoll ran to the window. He opened it. He leaned out. I quietly stepped to the card holder. I slipped the letter in my pocket. I put another letter back so he wouldn't miss it. I had made it just like his on the outside. I stepped over to the window.

"The noise in the street was made by a man who shot a gun into the air. It was a blank and hurt nobody. The police soon let him go. He was a man I'd paid to do that, of course. I talked a little longer with Divoll. Then I left."

"But why put another letter back?" I asked. "Why didn't you just take the letter and go?"

"Divoll is a brave man. He has plenty of nerve. He has his own men in the hotel. If I had tried that he'd have stopped me. I don't think I would have left that hotel alive. You would have heard no more of C. Auguste Dupin. But I had another idea, too. I'm for the Queen. For a long time Divoll has had her in his power. Now she has him. He still doesn't know the letter is gone. The next time the Queen will not help him. He will tell her he'll give the letter to the King. She'll laugh at him. He will get the letter out. He will look at it again. Then he's going to get an unhappy surprise."

"What do you mean? What did you put in the letter?"

"Well, I didn't want to put in a blank piece of paper. About five years ago Jacques Divoll did me a dirty trick. I wasn't very angry about it. But I told him then I'd never forget it. 'Someday, my friend,' I told him, 'I'm going to pay you back,' " I wanted him to know that I had taken the letter. So I just wrote him this little note:

A Jacques will never beat a queen
In games with
                    C. Auguste Dupin

THE GOLD BUG

Part I

MANY years ago I became friends with a Mr. William Legrand. He was a son of an old French family who had been very rich. But in one way and another Legrand had lost all his money. So he left his New Orleans home and moved to Sullivan's Island. Sullivan's Island is near Charleston, in South Carolina.

The island is about three miles long and a fourth of a mile wide. The trees and bushes are small. Old Fort Moultrie, built during the Revolutionary War, stands on the western side. Near the fort are a few empty frame houses. Most of the island is hard white sand thickly covered with small evergreen bushes.

Legrand built himself a little hut on the eastern side. It was there I first met him. As I saw him oftener, I got to like him. He was a well educated man. But he did not like people. Sometimes he would be gay and happy. The next time I'd see him he would be sad and gloomy. Then he would not speak at all.

He had many books in his little hut, but I never saw him reading. He liked to hunt and fish. Often he would walk along the shore looking for strange insects. He was much interested in them and knew a lot about them. With him went his simple old servant Jupiter. Legrand had no money to pay Jupiter, but the old man would not leave him.

Winters on Sullivan's Island are not very cold. During the fall a fire is needed only once in a great while. But one October day it grew very cold. Just before sunset I pushed through the evergreens to my friend's hut. I had not seen him for a few weeks. It wasn't too easy to get there in those days, for I lived about nine miles away in Charleston.

When I got to the hut, I knocked on the door. No answer. So I got the key from where Legrand kept it. I unlocked the door and went in. A big fire was burning in the fireplace. Cold as I was, I was glad to see it. I took off my overcoat and sat down.

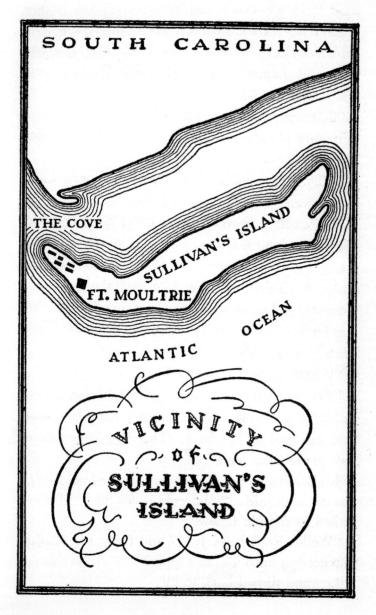

SOUTH CAROLINA

THE COVE

SULLIVAN'S ISLAND

FT. MOULTRIE

OCEAN

ATLANTIC

VICINITY OF SULLIVAN'S ISLAND

Soon after dark Legrand and Jupiter came in. Jupiter quickly started to cook supper. Legrand was feeling happy and was full of talk. He had found a new insect, a beetle.

"Tomorrow I want you to look at it," he said. "I'm sure it's a new kind. I know I've never seen it before."

"Why not tonight?" I asked, holding my hands to the fire.

"If I'd only known you were here!" said Legrand. "But it's so long since I saw you. How could I know you'd be here? As I was coming home I met Captain Smith, from the fort. I let him have the bug. He's interested in insects also. Stay here tonight. I'll send Jup for it in the morning. Oh, you'll be interested. It's a beautiful thing!"

"What? A beautiful bug?"

"Yes. It really is. It's a bright gold color. About as big as a hickory nut. There are two black spots near one end on the back. There's a longer black spot at the other end."

Jupiter looked up. "That bug is a real gold bug," the old man said. "Solid gold every bit of him." I smiled at the old fellow.

"Well, what if he is, Jup?" said Legrand. "Is that making you burn up the supper?"

Legrand turned back to me.

"You know," he said, "the bug has the color of real gold. It even shines like gold. Poor Jup thinks it is a gold bug. But you can see it yourself tomorrow. Here, I'll show you about how it looks."

Legrand sat down at a small table. He picked up a pen and the ink bottle. There was no paper on the desk. He looked in the drawer, but no paper was there either. He felt in his pockets.

"Never mind," he said, "this will do." And he pulled a piece of what looked like thick dirty paper from his vest pocket. He began to draw on it. I stayed in my chair near the fire, for I was still cold. Finally he finished the drawing. He handed it over to me. Just as I took it we heard a dog bark at the door. Jupiter opened the door. In jumped Legrand's big dog. I had always played with him on my visits, so he was glad to see me. He jumped at me and tried to lick my face. He was so big and heavy I almost backed into the fire. I held the drawing behind me to keep him from tearing it.

"Down, Prince," called Legrand.

When Prince sat down I looked at the drawing. I looked and looked at it again.

"Well," I said. "This is a strange looking bug. I never saw any bug like it. It looks like a skull to me."

"A skull?" said Legrand. "Oh, — yes — well, I guess it does. You mean the two black spots look like eyes? And the long spot at the other end looks like a mouth? And it is round."

"Maybe so. But I'd better wait till I see the bug, Legrand. I'm afraid you don't draw very well, my friend."

"Oh, I don't know about that. I should. I had good drawing teachers."

Legrand didn't seem to like what I'd said at all.

"Come, come, Legrand," I said. "You're just trying to be funny. This does look like a skull. I'd say it's a very good skull. Where are the bug's feelers?"

"The feelers? Can't you see them? I made them very plain. What's the matter with you?" Legrand was getting angry.

"Well," I answered, "maybe you did. Only I don't see them." I didn't want him angry with me so I gave him the paper. I was surprised at him. The drawing did look like a skull. And there were no feelers on the bug.

He grabbed the paper. I thought he was going to throw it into the fire. But he took one more look at it. Then he looked and looked again. He sat down and looked more carefully. At last he got up. He took a candle from the table. Then he walked to the end of the room. There he sat down on an old trunk. For a long time he studied the paper, turning it this way and that. Still he didn't say a word.

Finally he took his wallet from his coat pocket. Very carefully he put the paper inside. He put the wallet in his desk and locked it.

All the rest of the evening he was quiet. I tried to talk with him, but he would hardly answer. I even tried a few jokes. Again, no answer. I had wanted to stay with him that night. But when I saw how he was acting, I changed my mind. And he didn't ask me to stay, either. He shook hands in a very friendly way, though, and said good-night.

Part II

I didn't see Legrand for about a month. Then Jupiter came to see me. He seemed to be worried about Legrand. He was so sad that I began to wonder what was wrong.

"Well, Jup," I said. "What is the matter? How is Mr. Legrand?"

"I tell the truth, sir. He is not well. No sir, he's not well at all."

"Not well! I'm sorry to hear that. What's the matter with him?"

"He never tells me. But he's a very sick man."

"Very sick! Why didn't you tell me right away? Is he in bed?"

"No, he's not in bed. But he's sick. I'm worried about him."

"Jupiter, don't act so silly. Now what are you talking about? You say your master is sick. Hasn't he told you what's the matter with him?"

"Now don't be mad at me, sir. He walks with his head down. He don't talk. He just writes numbers on a paper all day."

"Numbers?"

"Yes, sir, numbers. And they're the funniest numbers I ever see. I got to watch him, too. He wants to get away from me. The other day he was gone before the sun was up. And he didn't come back all day. He looked awful white when he came back."

"You don't know how he got sick at all, Jupiter? Has he had bad news? Has anything happened since I saw him?"

"No, not *since* you did. It was the day you was there, sir."

"Why, what do you mean, Jup?"

"The bug, sir. That's it."

"The what?"

"The bug. That gold bug bit him. I know it."

"What makes you think so?"

"I saw him. He was a terrible bug. He kicked and he bit everything near him. Master Will caught him first, but he had to let him go. Bit him on the finger. I didn't like his looks. I wouldn't grab him with my bare hands. I found an old piece of paper

CAMROSE LUTHERAN COLLEGE
LIBRARY

PS
2615
694
A1

and picked him up with that. I stuffed a little part in his mouth. So he didn't bite me."

"You really think the bug bit your master? And that has made him sick?"

"I know it. Else why would he dream about the bug every night?"

"How do you know he dreams about it?"

"How do I know? Because he talks about it in his sleep. That's how I know."

"Well, Jup, maybe you're right. Did Mr. Legrand tell you to come to me?"

"Oh, yes, sir. He sent you a letter." Jupiter felt in his pockets and gave me this note:

Dear Edgar:

Why haven't you come to see me? I hope you aren't angry with me.

Something important has happened. I have something I want to tell you. I don't know just how to tell you. Maybe I shouldn't say anything at all.

I haven't been feeling very well. Old Jupiter gets in my way, trying to take care of me. He means well, but he isn't very bright, as you know.

Come back with Jupiter. Please come. I want to see you tonight. This is important.

Yours truly,
William Legrand

I didn't know what to think when I read the letter. Legrand didn't write letters that way. Could he be going crazy? What could be so important? Could Jupiter be right about him? I got ready to go back with Jupiter.

When I got into the boat to get to the island I stopped. In the boat were three new spades and a scythe for cutting grass and weeds.

"What are these for, Jup?" I asked.

"That's spades and a scythe."

"Yes, I know. But what are they doing here?"

"Master Will said to buy them. He gave me the money to get them."

"But what is he going to do with them?"

"That's more than I know. I bet he don't either. It's all that old gold bug that bit him." And old Jupiter shook his head sadly and pulled up the sail.

Part III

There was a strong wind, and in a little while we landed the boat just north of Fort Moultrie. A walk of two miles got us to the hut. We got there about three o'clock in the afternoon. Legrand was waiting for us eagerly. He grabbed my hand and shook it so hard that it hurt.

"I'm glad you came. I'm glad you came," he said.

I looked at him carefully. He was pale. His dark eyes shone with excitement.

"How are you, Legrand?"

"Fine, fine."

"You have been sick?"

"No, of course not. Feel fine."

"Say, did you ever get that gold bug back? The one you wanted to show me?"

"Yes. Got it back the next day. I wouldn't let it go again. Do you know Jupiter is right about that bug?"

Poor fellow, I thought. Something is wrong with him. "What do you mean?" I asked.

"He thinks it's really a gold bug. It is real gold to me."

Now I knew Jupiter must be right about Legrand. I looked at my friend sadly.

"This bug is going to make me a rich man again," he said, smiling. "Do you blame me for thinking a great deal of it? Lady Luck gave me this gold bug. All I've got to do is use it right and I'll be rich. Jupiter, bring me that bug!"

"What? What bug? No, sir, I just can't do it. Please!" And the old man just wouldn't touch it. Finally Legrand got up to get it himself. He had it in a glass case. It *was* a beautiful bug. At that time scientists did not know what it was, either. There were two round, black spots on one end of the back. One long spot was on the other end. The cover was hard and shining. It really did seem to be gold. I could not blame poor Jupiter for thinking it was. But I couldn't understand why Legrand would say it was gold. He knew better than that.

"I sent for you," Legrand said, "to help me. You—"

"Look, Legrand. You are a sick man. Get to bed. I'll stay with you a few days. You'll get over this. You have a fever—"

"Feel my head," said he.

I did. He had no fever.

"But you still may be sick. First, go to bed. Second, you—"

"No," he said. "You're wrong. I'm not sick. I'm just excited about something. If you really want to do something for me, you can."

"What do you want me to do?"

"Listen. Jupiter and I have to make a little trip. We need help. And I must be able to trust the one who helps. You are the only man I know I can trust."

"I'll help you any way I can. But tell me this. Has that gold bug got anything to do with the trip?"

"It has."

"Then, Legrand, I won't go. You're being silly."

"I'm sorry. We'll have to go alone then."

"Alone! Legrand, you must be crazy. Wait a

minute. How long do you think you will be gone?"

"All night. We start now. We'll be back by the time the sun rises."

"Will you promise me something? When we come back you will go to bed. And you will let me call a doctor."

"I promise."

"All right. I'll go along."

"Come on then. We have no time to lose."

Part IV

Slowly I went with my friend. We started about four o'clock. Legrand, Jupiter, Prince, the dog, and I all went. Jupiter carried the scythe and spades. Jup didn't want to go. He kept talking to himself all the way. We could hear him talk about "that old bug" and "that terrible bug." I carried the lanterns, Legrand had the gold bug. He had it tied to a string. He swung the bug around and wouldn't say a word to us. I tried to get him to tell where we were going.

"Just follow me," he said.

Then I tried to find out what we were going to do. But he just smiled.

"You'll see."

After a while we came to the northern end of the island. Here we took a little boat across the creek. Then we climbed to the high ground above the water.

Legrand led us toward the northwest. The country was very wild. We saw no one—not even a footstep. Legrand seemed to know just which way to go. Once in a while he stopped to look around him. I guessed he had come this way before and remembered some of the trees and rocks.

We went on for about two hours. Just as the sun went down we came to a wild and lonesome spot. It was a flat place on a hill. The sides of the hill were covered with trees and thick bushes. Here and there were big rough rocks. Deep valleys were all around us.

We climbed to the top and looked around. I now saw why Legrand had brought the scythe. The bushes were so thick and full of thorns we couldn't get through. Legrand pointed to a great tulip tree.

"Take the scythe, Jupiter," he said. "Cut us a path to the tree." The tulip tree was the biggest I had ever seen. It was much taller than the eight or ten oak trees near it. When we got to the tree Legrand looked at Jupiter.

"Can you climb that tree, Jup?" he asked.

The old man walked up to the tree. He walked around it slowly. Then he looked at the thick trunk.

"Yes, master. I can climb any tree I ever saw."

"Then get up. It will soon be too dark to see."

"How far up must I go?"

"Just get up the big trunk first. Then I'll tell you what to do. Here, wait. Take this bug with you."

"The bug! Master Will! Not that gold bug! Why must I take the gold bug?"

"Now, Jup, don't be afraid. A big man like you afraid of a little dead bug! Here, you can carry it by the string."

Jupiter put his hands behind him.

"Jup, you take this bug or I'll bang you on the head with this spade!"

"All right. All right. I was only fooling. I'm not afraid of that little old bug!"

Jupiter reached out very slowly and took hold of the string. He held it as far away as he could and got ready to climb.

Part V

A young tulip tree has a smooth trunk. It grows very tall and the branches are far above the ground. But as the tree gets older, the bark gets rough. Short branches then come out of the trunk. So the old tulip tree was not hard to climb. Jupiter held on to the big trunk with his arms and knees. He put his bare feet on the rough bumps in the bark. He nearly fell once or twice, but at last he got to the first big branch. From there on climbing was easy. He was about sixty or seventy feet from the ground.

"Which way now, Master Will?" he called.

"Keep going up. Stay on this side," answered Legrand.

The old man went up quickly now. Soon we couldn't see him any more. In a minute he called again.

"How much higher?"

"How high are you now?"

"Way up here. I can see the sky through the leaves."

"How many big branches have you passed? Count them on this side."

"One, two, three, four, five. I passed five branches, Master Will."

"Go up one more."

In a few minutes Jupiter called again.

"I passed six now, Master Will."

Legrand got excited.

"Now, Jup, listen carefully. Get out on that branch as far as you can. Let me know what you find."

Now I knew Legrand must be crazy. I began to wonder how I could get him home. While I was thinking, Jupiter's voice was heard again.

"I'm afraid to go out very far. It's a dead branch."

"Did you say a *dead* branch, Jup? Are you sure?"

"Yes, sir, it's dead."

"What am I going to do?" asked Legrand.

"Do?" I said. "Why, come home and go to bed.

Come on, Legrand. It's getting late. Remember your promise."

Legrand didn't even listen to me.

"Jupiter," he called, "do you hear me?"

"Yes, Master Will."

"Take your knife and cut the wood a little. See if it's very bad."

We heard nothing for a few minutes.

"It's dead, all right. Could be worse, though. Maybe I can go out a little way—by myself."

"By yourself! What do you mean?"

"Why, I mean the bug. It's a very heavy bug. If I drop the bug, I could go out alone. The branch won't break with just me."

Even Legrand had to laugh.

"Listen, Jup, you old fool. If you let that bug fall, I'm going to break your neck. Look here. Do you hear me?"

"Yes, Master Will, I can hear you."

"You get out on that branch and I'll give you a silver dollar when you get down. But you must take the bug."

"Yes, sir. Yes, sir. I'm going now. I'm near the end already."

"Near the end!" screamed Legrand. "Do you say you're near the end?"

"Soon be there. O-o-o-o-h! What is this?"

"Well," cried Legrand, "what is it that you see?"

"Why, it's nothing but a skull. Somebody left his head up here. Crows ate all the meat off."

"A skull, you say! Good! What's holding it on the tree?"

"Wait, I'll look. Say! There's a big nail in the skull. That's what holds it on the tree."

"Now, Jup, you do just what I tell you. Do you hear?"

"Yes, Master Will."

"Listen carefully. Find the left eye of the skull."

"Ha, ha, that's a good one. There's no left eye at all."

"Jupiter, don't be so dumb! Do you know which is your right hand?"

"Yes, Master Will. I chop wood with my left hand. My right hand is the other one."

"That's it. You are left handed. Your left eye is on the same side as your left hand. Now find the left eye of the skull. I mean find where the left eye *was*. Have you got it?"

There was no answer for a while. Jupiter was trying to figure it out. At last Jupiter asked, "Is the left eye of the skull on the same side as the left hand of the skull? The skull has no hand— never mind. I got it. Here's the left eye. What must I do with it?"

"Let the gold bug drop through it. But hold on to the string, now."

"All done. Here he goes. Watch it down there."

We couldn't see Jupiter at all. He was hidden by the leaves. But now we could see the bug. It hung from the end of the string. The sun was almost down, but it still shone on the bug. The bug was away from the branches. If Jupiter had let it go it would have fallen at our feet. Legrand took up the scythe. He quickly cut away the weeds and bushes below the bug.

"Let it go, Jup," he called. "Come on down."

Part VI

Legrand drove a stick into the ground where the bug landed. Then he took a tape measure from his pocket. He fastened one end to the tree trunk. He unrolled it till he reached the stick. Now he kept on going in a straight line. Jupiter kept ahead of him with the scythe, cutting the bushes away. When he had gone fifty feet Legrand stopped. Here he drove another stick into the ground.

"Clear away the bushes around the stick," he said to Jupiter. He picked up a spade himself and gave one to Jupiter and one to me.

"Dig," he said, and we set to work.

Now I don't like to dig. I was tired and night was coming on. But I couldn't see any way out. I

didn't want to get Legrand excited. If Jupiter would have helped, I would have made him go home. But I knew Jupiter wouldn't. I had guessed by now that Legrand must have heard one of the hundreds of old stories about buried treasure. Those stories were always being told. Most of us had stopped believing them long ago. I remembered what Legrand had said about the gold bug making him rich. The poor fellow, I thought, he surely has gone crazy. He thinks we're going to find a buried treasure. I made up my mind to stay with him until he found he was wrong. Then I'd take him home to bed.

It was now dark, so we lit the lanterns. The three of us went on digging. No one said a word. The dirt piled up as we went deeper and deeper. Prince started to jump in and out of the hole barking loudly. Legrand didn't want any one to come around so he tried to shut Prince up. No one was anywhere near that lonely place to bother us. Finally Jupiter took off his belt and tied the dog's mouth. That shut him up.

After two hours we were five feet deep. All we had found was dirt. We stopped a few minutes to rest. I began to hope Legrand would quit. He wasn't a very happy man, but he wiped the sweat from his head and started again. We now made the hole wider and two feet deeper. Still nothing. I began to feel sorry for Legrand. He climbed out of the hole without a word. Slowly he put on his coat. I said nothing. Jup said nothing. Legrand pointed to the scythe and spades. Jup picked them up. He took his belt from Prince. We turned and started home.

Part VII

We had taken about a dozen steps when Legrand let out a yell. He walked over to Jupiter and grabbed him by the collar. Old Jup dropped the scythe and spades. His mouth and eyes opened wide. Down he went to his knees.

"Jup, you answer me. Don't you lie. You tell me—which is your left eye?"

"Oh, my goodness, Master Will. Ain't this it?" And poor scared Jup put his finger on his *right* eye!

"I thought so! I knew it! Hurrah!" yelled Legrand. He let Jup go and jumped up and down with joy. Jupiter looked from him to me and back again.

"Come! We must go back," said Legrand. "We're not through yet." He led us back to the tulip tree.

"Jupiter, come here!" said Legrand when we reached the tree. "Was the skull looking away from the tree or toward the tree?"

"It was looking away from the tree. So the crows could get at it."

"Did you drop the bug through this eye or that one?" Here Legrand pointed to each of Jupiter's eyes.

"This eye, Master Will. The left eye." And Jupiter pointed to his *right* eye.

"That will do. We'll try it again."

I saw that Legrand knew what he was doing. Maybe, I thought, he isn't so crazy after all. He pulled out the stick where the bug had fallen. Then he moved it about three inches west. Now he got out his tape measure again. As before, he fastened it to the trunk. He unrolled it to the stick and kept going. When he had gone fifty feet he stopped again and drove a stick into the ground. The new spot was a few yards away from where we had been digging.

Jupiter cut away the bushes again, we took our spades, and we started to dig. I was very tired by now, but I made the dirt fly. Legrand seemed to know what he was doing. Maybe we would find treasure! I began to get excited. After we had dug for an hour and a half, Prince began barking again. The first time he had just wanted to play. But now something else was wrong. Jupiter took his belt again and tried to tie his mouth. Prince got away and jumped into the hole. To our surprise, he began to dig. Soon he uncovered a pile of human bones.

We pulled Prince away and we saw the bones were two whole skeletons. Legrand dug a little deeper and found a large blade from an old Spanish knife. Jupiter and I began to help. Next we turned up three or four old gold coins.

Jupiter fell to his knees and grabbed them happily, But Legrand said nothing about them.

"Keep digging," he told us.

All at once I fell forward. I looked to see what had made me fall. A large iron ring was sticking out of the ground. I had caught my toe in it and stumbled. We tried to pull it up, but it was fastened to something large and heavy.

Now we really got to work. Never have I had ten minutes of greater excitement. We cleared away the dirt and uncovered an old wooden chest. It was not rotted a bit and was wonderfully hard. Legrand guessed something had been put on the wood to keep it from rotting. This box was three and a half feet long, three feet wide, and two and a half feet deep. It had heavy iron bands all around it. On both sides, near the top were three iron rings — six in all. They were put on so six men could get a good hold to carry it. Legrand, Jupiter, and I got hold and pulled. We couldn't even move it. We looked to see how the lid was fastened. Only two sliding bolts! We pulled them back, breathing hard. Legrand threw back the lid. Before our eyes lay a great treasure! The lanterns shone on a pile of gold and jewels which almost blinded us.

I can't really tell you how we felt. I thought I'd been hit on the head. Legrand was worn out and said little. Jupiter's mouth hung wide open. He couldn't believe what his eyes saw. Finally he fell on his knees at the chest. He pushed his bare arms into the gold to his elbows. There he stayed, as if he were taking a bath in it. When he could talk we heard him say:

"And this comes from the gold bug! The pretty gold bug! The poor little gold bug I didn't like.

Jupiter, you should be ashamed of yourself! Lucky, lucky gold bug!"

Part VIII

Well, we had the job of getting the treasure home. It was getting late. We wanted to get it put away before morning. It was hard to get started. None of us knew what to do first. Finally we took about two-thirds of the gold and jewels out of the box. Then we were able to lift it from the hole. Among the bushes we hid the part we had taken out. Prince was left to guard it. Jupiter told the dog to be quiet and not to move. We then hurried home with the chest. We got to Legrand's hut at about one o'clock in the morning. Our legs just wouldn't move. So we rested until two and had supper. As soon as we finished we started back. This time we each carried a big strong sack. We got back a little before four. Now we each filled our sacks. The hole we left unfilled. We were back at the hut just as the sun came up.

Now we were really worn out. Into the beds we fell. I guess we were too excited to sleep long, though. After three or four hours we were up again. We wanted to see just what we did have.

The chest had been full to the top. We spent the whole day and most of the next night going over the treasure. Everything was mixed up together.

Whoever filled the chest had just thrown one thing in on the other. When we counted what was there, we had more than we had thought at first. In money alone—gold coins—there was more than four hundred and fifty thousand dollars. We had to guess how much some of the coins were worth. All were old. There was not one bit of silver. There were French, Spanish, German, and English coins. There were even some we'd never seen or heard of. Some of the big gold coins were so old the writing had been worn off them. Not one piece of American money was in the chest. We had a harder time figuring out how much the jewels were worth. There were a hundred and ten fine large diamonds. We found eighteen beautiful rubies. Three hundred and ten emeralds were counted. There were also twenty-one sapphires and one opal. These jewels had all been torn from their gold settings and thrown loose in the chest. The settings had been beaten up with hammers. Legrand thought that was done so the real owners would never know them again. But that wasn't all. There were a lot of solid gold ornaments. There were nearly two hundred gold finger rings and ear rings. I remember thirty gold chains and eighty-three heavy gold crosses. I think there were five big golden dishes and a large bowl. Legrand liked the two beautiful sword handles.

There were many other smaller things which I don't remember any more. Besides, we found one hundred and ninety-seven big beautiful gold watches. Three of them sold for five hundred dollars each. Many of them were very old and their wheels had rusted. They couldn't be used, but their cases were fine gold with jewels in them. We guessed that the whole chest full was worth about a million and a half dollars. When we sold the gold and jewels later, we found it worth much more.

Part IX

At last we got through counting. I couldn't wait any longer to hear how Legrand had found out about the treasure. He smiled at me.

"I know you want to hear all about it," he said.

"Yes, I do. I'm not going to let you do another thing until you tell me."

We sat down before the fire and he began.

"You remember the night I made the drawing of the gold bug. I was angry because you said I'd drawn a skull. At first I thought you were joking. But then I thought of the bug's black spots. Well, I thought, those could look like eyes. Still, I was angry. I always thought I could draw pretty well. When you gave me the piece of parchment I was going to throw it away."

"The piece of paper, you mean," said I.

"No. It looked like paper. I thought it was paper, too. But when I started to draw on it I saw it was parchment."

"What's the difference?"

"Why, parchment, you know, is made from sheep or goat skin. It's much tougher than paper. Years ago people used it a lot. Any writing they wanted to keep, they put on parchment. It lasted much longer than paper."

"Go on."

"Well, it was dirty. Just as I was going to throw it away, I looked at it. I got a surprise. I saw a skull. But I hadn't drawn that skull. I had drawn a bug. And here, in the same place, was a skull instead of my bug! For a minute I couldn't think. I picked up a candle and sat down on that trunk over there. I looked at it carefully. I turned it over. And there on the other side was my bug! The bug was just about as big as the skull. They were both round. The skull was near the top of the parchment. So was the bug, on the other side. For a few minutes I just couldn't figure it out. But then I remembered something! When I drew the bug, there was *nothing* on the other side. I was sure of this. For I had turned the parchment over, looking for the cleanest side. If the skull had been there, I would have seen it. I wanted time to think about it. So I got up and put the parchment away. I was going to think it over alone.

"That night when you were gone and Jupiter was asleep I did so. First, I tried to remember how I got the parchment. We found the bug on the shore. It was in the sand, not far from the water. I picked it up, but it bit me. I dropped it near Jupiter. He looked for a leaf to pick it up. We both saw this piece of parchment. Just one part was sticking out of the sand. I remember seeing the wreck of a ship's life-saving boat near by. It must have been there a long time. I had to look twice before I could tell it had been a boat.

"Well, Jupiter picked up the parchment. He put the bug in it and gave it to me. A little later we went home. On the way we met Captain Smith. I showed the Captain the gold bug. He wanted to look at it, so I let him take it home. He put it into his pocket. I guess he was afraid I'd change my mind. So we started for the fort right away. I must have just put the parchment into my pocket then.

"You remember that I was going to draw the bug. When I looked on the table, there was no paper. I looked in the drawer, but none was there either. Then I felt in my pockets. I thought I might have an old letter there. That's when I found the parchment again.

"I was already on the right track then. Two things fitted together. First, there was an old boat on the shore. Second, not far from the boat was a parchment. Remember—parchment, and *not a paper*, with a skull on it."

"I don't see what a boat has to do with the parchment," I said. "Why get excited about a skull?"

"Did you ever see a pirate's flag?"

"Why, I guess every boy sometime has drawn a pirate flag."

"What's on it?"

"A skull and two bones across each other."

"That's right."

"You thought the boat was a pirate's?"

"It was a pretty good guess, wasn't it?"

"And that the parchment once belonged to a pirate?"

"Yes. A pirate would likely put a skull and crossed bones over anything he wrote."

"I guess he would."

"I said the skull was on parchment, and not paper. Parchment lasts a long time. Anything not important wouldn't be put on parchment. Paper is much easier to write on. I guessed that a pirate had written something very important on that parchment. And it must have been something he wanted to keep a long, long time."

Part X

"But, Legrand," I said, "when you drew the bug the skull wasn't there. The skull must have been made *after* the bug. Who did it? When was it done? And what could the skull then have to do with the old boat?"

"That was the big mystery. But I didn't have much trouble there. Here's the way I figured. When I drew the bug, there was no skull. I gave you the parchment. You just looked at it and gave it back. You couldn't have drawn the skull. I didn't draw it. But there it was."

"Then I tried to remember just what had happened. The weather was cold that day. And it was lucky for us it was! We had a big fire going. I had been out walking and was warm. So I sat away from the fire over there. You were cold. So you sat close to the fire over here. I gave you the parchment. Just as you looked at it, Prince came in. He jumped up at you. You held him off with your left hand. Your right hand held the parchment. You held it away from Prince, close to the fire. I remember it almost caught fire. I was going to say something, but then Prince lay down. Then you looked at it again. Now what had happened to that parchment while you had it?"

"Why, it must have been heated."

"Right. The heat must have brought out the skull. Now, you know there is such a thing as invisible ink. There are different kinds. They have been used for hundreds of years. They are green, red, and other colors. After you write, the ink becomes invisible. When you heat the paper, the writing can be seen again.

"Now I looked at the skull carefully. The outer parts were much clearer than the others. I could guess why that was. Some parts of the parchment had got more heat than others. So I got the fire going again. Then I heated the parchment all over. At first only the skull got clearer. But as I kept heating it, I could see something on the bottom. It got clearer and clearer. At last I could make out what I thought was a goat.

"A goat?"

"I looked closer and found it was a young goat— a kid."

"Ha! Ha!" said I. "And what have pirates to do with goats?"

"But I just told you it was *not* a goat."

"Well, a kid, then. Pretty much the same thing."

"Pretty much, yes. But still not the same. Especially when you think of Captain Kidd, the famous pirate."

"Right you are, Legrand. I missed that one."

"The kid was at the bottom of the parchment. I thought it could be there in place of the name. If Captain Kidd wanted to write something, that's about what he'd do. He'd put the skull at the top and his name at the bottom. Why shouldn't he draw a kid if his name was Kidd?"

"Then I guess you looked for a letter between the skull and the kid?"

"Something like that. You've heard the old stories of buried treasure around here, haven't you?"

"Hundreds of them."

"Well, they all say the treasure was hidden on the Atlantic coast somewhere. Kidd and his pirates did sail around here long ago. You've heard these old stories. But did you ever hear that someone found treasure?"

"No, I never did."

"Neither did I. I thought there must be some truth to them. Kidd did bury treasure. Kidd was around here. Nobody ever found it. So maybe the treasure was still buried."

"But why wouldn't Captain Kidd come back for it?"

"Maybe he couldn't. Maybe he couldn't find the place again. This is a big coast and the country is wild. He'd hide it very carefully to be sure it was safe. Maybe he wrote down how to find the place again. That's just about what he would do. And suppose he lost the directions? There are a lot of reasons."

"And you thought—"

"Yes. I thought this parchment might be the directions for finding the treasure."

"Well, I guess you were right. What did you do next?"

Part XI

"I held the parchment to the fire again. Then I tried to give it more heat. But I couldn't get anything else to show. I wondered if the dirt had anything to do with it. So I cleaned it. I poured warm water over the parchment. Then I put it in a pan of water. I set the pan over the fire. After a few minutes I took it up again. Now I began to see some spots. Looking closely, I saw that they were lines of numbers. I put the parchment back in the pan and left it there another minute. I'll show you what I saw then."

Here Legrand put the parchment in the pan again and heated it. After a few minutes he pulled it out and showed it to me. This is what I saw, written in red ink.

5 3 ‡ ‡ † 3 0 5)) 6 * ; 4 8 2 6) 4 ‡ .) 4 ‡) 8 0
6 * ; 4 8 † 8 ¶ 6 0)) 8 5 ; ;] 8 * ; : ‡ * 8 † 8
3 (8 8) 5 * † ; 4 6 (; 8 8 * 9 6 * ? ; 8) * ‡ (; 4 8

5) ; 5 * † 2 : * ‡ (; 4 9 5 6 * 2 (5 * — 4) 8 ¶ 8
* ; 4 0 6 9 2 8 5) ;) 6 † 8) 4 ‡ ‡ ; 1 (‡ 9 ; 4 8
0 8 1 ; 8 : 8 ‡ 1 ; 4 8 † 8 5 ; 4) 4 8 5 † 5 2 8 8 0
6 * 8 1 (‡ 9 ; 4 8 ; (8 8 ; 4 (‡ ? 3 4 ; 4 8) 4
‡ ; 1 6 1 ; : 1 8 8 ; ‡ ? ;

"But what does it mean?"

"Well, that wasn't very hard to figure out. It looks harder than it is. This is a code. It means something. I didn't think Captain Kidd could make a very hard code. It looked like an easy one to me. But Kidd, I guess, thought no one would be able to figure it out."

"And you really figured it out yourself?"

"Yes, very easily. I have done much harder ones. You see, I have always been interested in codes. I don't think any one can make a code that can't be broken. The hardest part for me was making the numbers plain enough to be seen.

"The first thing to find out was the *language* used. You can't work a code in French as you do in English. Every language is different. But I had the answer to that, too. The code was English."

"But how could you tell, Legrand?"

"By the drawing of the kid. The words for "kid" in all other languages don't sound like "Kidd" at all. The drawing makes sense only in English."

Part XII

"You see all the numbers are run together. They aren't broken up into words. If the code showed where the words began and ended, it would have been very easy."

"How would that have helped you?"

"I would have looked for a word that had only one letter first. That would have been "a" or "I." I would have tried these letters out in other short words. From these I could guess other letters."

"I see. But you couldn't do that, could you?"

"No. The first thing I did was to find which of the code figures were used most. I made a list of them. Here is the list I made."

Legrand handed me a piece of paper. This is what he had written.

The figure 8 is in the code 34 times.

The figure ; is in the code 27 times.

The figure 4 is in the code 19 times.

The figure) is in the code 16 times.

The figure ‡ is in the code 15 times.

The figure * is in the code 14 times.

The figure 5 is in the code 12 times.

The figure 6 is in the code 11 times.

The figure (is in the code 9 times.

The figure † is in the code 8 times.

The figure 1 is in the code 7 times.

The figure 0 is in the code 6 times.
The figure 2 is in the code 5 times.
The figure 9 is in the code 5 times.
The figure 3 is in the code 4 times.
The figure : is in the code 4 times.
The figure ? is in the code 3 times.
The figure ¶ is in the code 2 times.
The figure — is in the code 1 time.
The figure . is in the code 1 time.
The figure] is in the code 1 time.

"Why did you do that?"

"In English, the letter that comes most often is *e*. After *e* they go like this: a o i d h n r s t u y c f g l m w b k p q x z. But the letter *e* is far ahead of the others. It comes far oftener than any other letter.

"So here I had something to work on. There are more of the figure 8 in the code than any other figure. So I guessed that 8 stands for *e*. I made another test to see if that was right."

"How did you do that?"

"You know that in English we have many double *e*'s in our words. Think of 'meet,' 'fleet,' 'speed,' 'seen.' "

"Say, that's right—'been,' 'deed,' 'seed,' 'feed.' "

"Yes, and many more. If you look at the parchment you'll see the 8's together five times."

I looked at the parchment. I counted them off like this:

53‡‡†305))6*;4826)4‡.)4‡)80
6*;48†8¶60))85;;]8*;:‡*8†8
8((88)⁴)5*†;46(;88²*96*?;8)*‡(;48
5);5*†2:*‡(;4956*2(5*—4)8¶8
*;4069285);)6†8)4‡‡;1(‡9;48
081;8:8‡1;48†85;4)485†52(88)³0
6*81(‡9;48;((88)⁴;4(‡?34;48)4
‡;161;:1(88)⁵;‡?;

"All right," I said. "Even I can see that the 8 must be *e*. What next?"

"Well, the *word* that comes most often in English is 'the.' Let's look at the two figures in front of the 8's. If the same two figures come before the 8 a few times—"

"The first will be *t* and the second will be *h*?"

"That's right. Let's see if we can't find the same figures before the 8."

We picked up the parchment again and looked. I marked off the figures like this:

53‡‡†305))6*;(;48)26)4‡.)4‡();8)0
6*(;48)†8¶60())8)5;(;]8)*;:(‡*8)†.8
(3(8)8)5*†;46((;8)8*96*(?;8))*‡((;48)
5);5*†2:*‡(;4956*2(5*—(4)8¶8
*;4069285);)(6†8))4‡‡;1(‡9(;48)
08(1;8):8‡1(;48)†85;4()48)5†(528)80
(6*8)1(‡9(;48)(;(8)8;4(‡?34(;48))4
‡;161;(:18)8;‡?;

91

"Well," said Legrand, "do you see which two figures come most often before the 8?"

"Wait a minute," I said, "I've got it. Here they are—" and I wrote

; 48.

"Now," said Legrand, "I knew that the; stood for *t* and the 4 stood for *h*."

"But how can you get the other letters?"

"I'll show you. When you get one word, you can use it to find the beginning or ending of other words. Look at the second last ; 48."

"Here it is."

"Write them."

I wrote:

; 48.

"Now write the next six figures after that."

I did. Now I had written this:

; 48 ; (88; 4

"Now," said Legrand, "how many of those figures do we know?"

I looked at the paper.

"All but one."

"Write the letters in place of the figures. Skip the one you don't know."

So I wrote:

thet eeth

"It doesn't make sense," I said.

"Wait a minute. The first 'the' is a word, isn't it?"

"Yes."

"What have you got left when you take it away?"

I wrote:

t eeth

"Can you find a letter to put in after the *t* to make sense?"

I tried every letter. Not one would make a word. I tried again, to be sure.

"There is no letter that will fit there, Legrand," I said.

"Well, if no letter will fit, that isn't a word. Try knocking off the last *th*. Write what's left."

I wrote:

t ee

"Now try all your letters again," said Legrand.

I tried every letter from *a* to *z*.

"I've got it! It must be 'tree'."

"That's right. Now you know another letter—*r*. You'd better write down the ones you know."

I wrote:

$$; = t$$
$$4 = h$$
$$8 = e$$
$$(= r$$

"Now," said Legrand, "write the part you just

got over again. Then keep going. Write the next ten figures."

So now I wrote this:

> ; 48 ; (88 ; 4 (‡ ? 34; 48

"We know most of these, Legrand."

"Then write them in."

Again I wrote:

the tree thr‡?3h the

"Can you guess that word?" asked Legrand.

"Well," I said slowly, "I'm not sure."

"Try writing the word with dots for the letters you don't know."

I did so:

thr . . . h

"Looks like 'through'," I said.

"And that's just what it is. Now you know three more letters—*o, u,* and *g*."

"I'll write them with the others I know." My paper now looked like this:

; = t		‡ = o
4 = h		? = u
8 = e		3 = g
(= r		

"Here's another good spot to work on," said Legrand. He took the pencil and copied this from the parchment—

> 83 (88

94

"Looking at your paper," he said; "we can put in the letters we know. That would make

egree

"That looks like 'degree'," I said.

"A good guess. The figure for *d* is †. You can add that to your paper. Now look four figures after 'degree.' You see this—

; 46 (; 88 *

"Let's put in the ones we know. We'll put dots for the ones we don't know." So he wrote the letters and dots:

th . rtee.

"You can guess that one too. It looks like 'thirteen', doesn't it? And now you have two more letters. The 6 stands for *i* and the * for *n*. Let's do one more. Look at the first five figures in the top line. Write them."

I wrote:

5 3 ‡ ‡ †

Then I put in the ones we knew and got this:

5 good

"I know," I said. "The 5 is one letter. A one-letter word in English would be *I* or *a*. 'I good' doesn't make sense, so the 5 stands for a."

"That's the way to do it. Let's see how many letters you've got now."

I added the new ones to the others. My paper now looked like this:

; = t	‡ = o	6 = i
4 = h	? = u	* = n
8 = e	3 = g	5 = a
(= r	† = d	

"You have eleven letters there," said Legrand. "We won't have to do them all again. I just wanted you to see how it can be done. Not hard, is it?"

"No, not when you know how."

"Here's the way it works out. When I finished, this is what I had:

" 'A good glass in the bishop's hostel in the devil's seat twenty-one degrees and thirteen minutes northeast and by north main branch seventh limb east side shoot from the left eye of the death's-head a bee line from the tree through the shot fifty feet out.' "

Part XIII

"What on earth does that mean? I can't make any sense out of that! What's a 'devil's seat'? What's a 'death's head'? And a 'bishop's hostel'?"

"It looks hard," agreed Legrand. "First, I tried to break it into parts. The man who wrote this tried to make it hard by running it together.

"Well, I just cut it up like this:

" 'A good glass in the Bishop's hostel in the devil's

96

seat — twenty-one degrees and thirteen minutes — northeast and by north — main branch seventh limb east side — shoot from the left eye of the death's head — a bee-line from the tree through the shot fifty feet out.' "

"I still don't know what it means," I said.

"I didn't either," said Legrand. "So I tried to find out. I walked around near Sullivan's Island and asked questions. Now you know that 'hostel' is an old word for 'hotel.' So I asked people if they knew anything about 'Bishop's Hotel.' No one knew. I kept wondering about it. At last I remembered that an old family named Bessop long lived here. They lived in an old house about four miles north of the island. 'Bessop' sounds like 'Bishop,' so I tried it. I walked over to the old house and talked to the oldest people I could find around there. One of the oldest women told me she remembered hearing of a Bessop's Castle. She said it was nothing but a high rock. 'Can you show me where it is?' I asked. She said she could if she could walk that far.

"I told her I'd pay her well. She didn't want to come, but at last she did. We got there without any trouble. I paid her and told her to go back home. I looked around carefully. The 'castle' was a lot of cliffs and rocks. One rock was much taller than the others. I climbed to the top and sat down. I needed to catch my breath. I didn't know what to do next.

"I looked around me. About a yard below me I saw a flat place that looked something like a seat. I leaned over and saw it had a back to it. The rock looked like an old chair. 'Oh,' I said to myself, 'I'll bet that's the devil's seat.'

"Now I had the 'Bishop's hotel' and the 'devil's seat.' A good glass in the Bishop's hotel in the 'devil's seat.' Then I remembered something. A sailor calls a telescope a 'glass.' I should sit in the devil's seat and look through a telescope, or glass. I knew that was right. The next part of the code read 'twenty-one degrees and thirteen minutes.' That meant how high to hold the glass. And 'northeast and by north' meant the direction to hold the glass. Very much excited, I hurried home. I got out my telescope and went back to the rock.

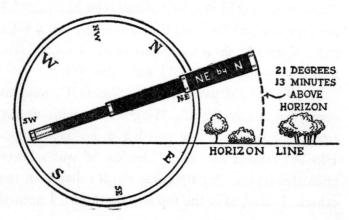

"I climbed down to the seat. I found I could look only one way when I sat down. I got out my compass and laid it beside me. Now I got the right direction. I raised the telescope. I had to guess at the twenty-one degrees. Slowly I moved the telescope up and down. Through the telescope I saw a large tree. I looked at it closely. There was a big bare spot where no leaves grew. In the middle I saw something white. I rubbed my eyes and looked again. Then I saw what it was—a skull!

"Then I did get excited. I was sure I had the secret. The words 'main branch, seventh limb, east side' meant where the skull was. I could now guess what the rest meant, too. 'Shoot from the left eye of the death's head' could mean only one thing. I had to drop a bullet through the left eye of the skull. A 'beeline' means a straight line. I was to draw a straight line from the tree through the place where the bullet dropped. Then I had to keep going fifty feet. There would be the spot to dig. I was sure there would be buried treasure.'

"I see," said I. "It all sounds easy now. What did you do when you left the Bishop's Hotel?"

"I looked carefully so I could find the big tree later. Just as soon as I got up, I couldn't see the bare spot any more. I turned this way and that. But it was gone. The strange thing is that you can see that one bare spot only from the 'devil's seat.' "

"Jupiter had gone with me to the Bishop's Hotel. I didn't tell him what I was doing. He thought I was going crazy. I guess I looked crazy, all right. Jupiter watched me and stayed close to me all day. The next morning I got up early. I kept quiet so I wouldn't wake him. I went out to find the tree. After a long search I found it. You know the rest of the story."

"We missed the right spot because Jupiter had the wrong eye, didn't we?"

"Yes. The right spot for the bullet was only three inches away. If we were to dig there, it would not have made any difference. But when you run a straight line fifty feet farther, you get away from the right spot. Look—"

Here Legrand got a piece of paper and a pen. He made this drawing.

"Here you can see why the wrong eye made us dig for nothing," said Legrand.

"Captain Kidd didn't have to use a skull, did he? Was that just because he was a pirate?"

"Maybe. But remember this. He had to have something you could see from the 'devil's seat.' So the thing had to be *white*. And it had to *stay* white. Kidd didn't know when he'd come back. Maybe he would have to send someone to get his treasure. Now what could he use? The thing would have to be out in the weather for years. A skull or bones get whiter the older they grow. So a skull was the best thing he could use."

"But you, Legrand! The way you marched along with your old bug! Why did you use the bug instead of a bullet? Jupiter could have dropped a bullet."

"I'll tell you why. You were so sure I was going crazy! And you kept trying to make me go to bed. I thought I'd play a little joke on you. I wanted to teach you a lesson. The bug was heavy and it didn't make any difference. It landed the same place a bullet would have landed."

"I see. There's one more thing I'd like to know. Why were the skeletons in the hole?"

"We can only guess that. But I'm sure I know what happened. Captain Kidd must have been a hard man. And you know dead men tell no tales.

Kidd couldn't carry that chest alone. He needed some men to help. Any man who helped might remember where the treasure was buried. So, while the men were in the hole—Kidd standing above them—a few swift blows with an ax. Who knows?"

SECRET MESSAGES

YOU were probably interested in the secret message which Legrand worked out. People have studied secret ways of writing for thousands of years. The study of secret writing is called *cryptography*. Our word *cryptography* comes from two Greek words. The Greek word *kryptos* meant "secret." The Greek word *graphein* meant "to write." We have made one word out of the two. So, *cryptography* means "secret writing."

Cryptography is useful in time of war. Messages are sent from one commander to another. The enemy tries to get the message and figure it out.

Government workers in foreign lands often send information back home in this way. Business men sometimes use a code to write to one another. Even tramps have a secret way of writing. They sometimes write information on fences with chalk. In this way other tramps can tell whether a family may give them a meal.

Long ago the Spartans used a clever way of sending secret messages in war time. Suppose a Spartan general wanted to send a letter to another general. He would first wrap a parchment ribbon at a slant around a round stick. Then he wrote his letter. He took it off the stick and folded it. A soldier then took it to the other general. This general had a round stick exactly like the first one. When he wrapped the parchment around his stick at the same slant, he could read the message. Sometimes the enemy caught the messenger. But they couldn't read the message. They didn't know how thick the stick had to be and they didn't know the right slant at which to wrap the parchment.

Here is another clever trick a Greek worked long ago. He was in the enemy's country and wanted to send a secret message home. Of course, he didn't want anyone else to get the message. He shaved the head of his faithful slave. Then he tattooed the message on the slave's head. He waited until the hair grew back. The slave was to say, "Shave my head and look at it," when he got home. His friend got the message. The same idea was used in the First World War. Spies with messages in invisible ink on their skins often crossed the enemy's lines.

Friends of prisoners have been able to get messages past prison guards. Here is an old story about Sir John Trevanion. Sir John had fought against Cromwell and for King Charles of England. When Cromwell became ruler, he threw Charles' friends into prison. Cromwell locked Sir John up in an old castle. John and his friends knew that he would soon be killed. But one day the guard gave him a letter. John reached for it eagerly.

"It won't do you any good," said the guard. "The letter was read carefully by the jailer."

The letter went something like this:

Dear John:

Hope, that is the best comfort, cannot, I fear, help you now. What I say, is this. If ever I can do something for you, state what it is. 'Tis not much I can do. But, feel sure I am willing. I know that, if death comes, tho others are afraid, it frightens you not a bit. Face it bravely. We had no braver soldier than you. Pray every day that they will spare you. Hope for the best. I fear I can do little. Only do think well of me. 'Tis not in my power to help you much. Tell me what I may do, or if not for you, old friend, then for your family. Best wishes.

R. T.

But Sir John knew how to find the real message in the letter. He read the third letter after every punctuation mark—the third letter after a colon, or a comma, or a period. If you do what Sir John did, you will get the message:

PANEL AT EAST END OF CHAPEL SLIDES.

Sir John asked to go to the chapel to pray. The jailer let him go. When they came to get him, you may be sure Sir John was miles away.

The invisible ink which Captain Kidd used is an old story, too. If you don't want to keep a secret message long you can make your ink from milk, sugar, and water. You can see the writing for a little while only, though. You must hold the paper over the flame of an oil lamp until it nearly scorches. Another simple way to make invisible ink is to put iodine on starch. The ink is blue and fades when it is dry. You can make it come back by heating the paper.

Years ago a band of Russians were fighting against their ruler. These men wrote to one another using invisible ink. They would write harmless letters and leave a wide space between the lines. Then they would write the real message with invisible ink between the lines.

The government men soon caught on to this. They got some of the letters and heated them to bring the writing back. But the writers soon took care of that. They wrote letters as before, leaving wide spaces between the lines. Now they put gun cotton on the paper. They made sure the letters would be caught. When the government men heated the paper, it blew up in their faces.

On the following pages are some of the ways secret messages have been written.

Forward or Backward

Here is a simple way to write secret messages. Can you read this?

Uijt   pof   jt   fbtz   jt   ju   opu?

The letter which follows the correct one has always been written instead of the letter itself. So, B is written for A, C is written for B, D is written for C, and so on. This one is easy, is it not?

Another easy way is to use the letter which comes before the letter you would usually write. So, instead of A, write Z; instead of B, write A; instead of C, write B; instead of D, write C. You will find this easy to read.

Dcfzq   Zkkzm   Ond   vqnsd   sgd   Fnkc   Atf

Squares and Triangles

Here is another old way to write a different alphabet. You will be able to learn the new alphabet easily. Just learn how the letters are made. You first draw these lines like this:

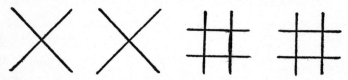

Now put dots in the figures like this:

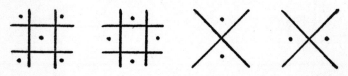

Now put the letters into each empty space like this:

Now make the parts of the figures stand alone:

Now you can read this message:

More Squares and Triangles

A still easier one is much like the one you have just learned. It has been used for hundreds of years. Perhaps you can remember it more easily than the other one.

See if you can find out what this message says:

[cipher symbols]

First, Middle, and Last

Here is another easy one. The letters which make up the real words are written at the beginning, in the middle, and at the end of a word you invent. Suppose you want to write "man." You write:

M

because the first letter counts. Now mix in any letters that will mean nothing:

Mel

Now add the next real letter to what you have:

Mela

Add any two other letters. For example:

Melabi

Now add the last one, which counts:

Melabin

The first letter counts and is M
The middle letter counts and is A
The last letter counts and is N

You can also write "man" like this: Mxakn

Or like this: Mukzapyon

110

This code does not keep words apart from one another. The one who reads the message must figure out where one word ends and another begins.

Now you can read this message:

Rxeba   dotth   imkstac   azbirpete   fuuyl   ly

Turn Them Around

This one is an easy code to remember. Two boys at school invented it and used it for a long time. The other boys could not figure it out. See if you can get it before you look below for the answer.

PIKSE EHTE TSALE SRETTELE DNAE
DAERE EHTE SDROWE SDRAWKCABE

The boys just wrote all the words backwards and added an E to the end of every word. You read the message by taking off the last "E" and writing the letters from right to left.

A Dictionary Code

A dictionary code is another easy one. First, you agree with a friend on which dictionary you will use. Now write your message. Look up your first word in this dictionary. Write down the page number. Then write the column number. Last, write the number of the word. For example, 37-2-10 means page 37, column 2, tenth word. Do the same for the other words. Now your message is written in numbers. When your friend gets the message, he takes out his dictionary and finds the words. To read the message, you must know which dictionary is being used.

You can use the same idea with any book. Just write the page and word number. If you wish to write words, you may use the word before or after the right word in the dictionary.

A Box Code

Write your alphabet in boxes like this:

A	B
C	D

E	G
F	H

I	J
K	L

M	N
O	P

Q	R
S	T

U	V
W	Y

The one who gets the message must have the letters in boxes the same way. The two letters X and Z are not in the boxes. If you need X or Z in your message, just write X or Z. Now, instead of writing the real letter, use the one in the same square of the opposite box. If you need "a," write "e." If you need "k," use "o." If you need "v," write "r." If you need "h," use "d."

Suppose you want to write "Treasure is hidden."
Using this box code you would write this:

YVAEWQVA   MW   DMHHAJ

You can read this, can't you?

WAGVAY   IAWWECA

Typewriter Code

This is the way the letters follow on a typewriter:

A	B	C	D	E	F	G	H	I	J
Q	W	E	R	T	Y	U	I	O	P

K	L	M	N	O	P	Q	R	S
A	S	D	F	G	H	J	K	L

T	U	V	W	X	Y	Z
Z	X	C	V	B	N	M

In the typewriter code you let Q stand for A, W
for B, E for C, R for D and so on down the line.

Here is a way you can read and write such messages quickly. Print the 26 letters of the alphabet
on little circles of paper. Now paste the A circle on
the Q typewriter key. Paste the B on the W key.
Paste the C on the E key. Paste the rest of the letters
on the right keys. Now you can type out your message. The typewriter will write in code.

The one who gets the message may also paste the
paper letters on his typewriter keys. If he now copies
your secret message, the typewriter will write the
real message.

Paste the letters on a typewriter. Then copy this

secret message and read what the typewriter writes.

QD   O   FGZ   Q   LDQKZ   ZNHTVKOZTK

A Dot Code

Make a key like this on a typewriter with one space between letters. Cut it out along the dotted lines.

. . . .

. A B C D E F G H I J K L M N O P Q R S T U V W X Y Z .

. . . .

Now lay it on a sheet of paper just as wide as the key. You are ready to write your message. Put a dot under the first letter of your first word. Now put a dot under the second letter of your first word but make the dot a little lower than the first one. Go on like this until you have a dot for every letter of every word in your message. Be sure to make each dot a little lower than the one before.

The one who gets the message must have a key like yours. When he gets the message, he lays his key on the paper. He can then see which letters are meant by each dot.

Can you read this message?

Key

A B C D E F G H I J K L M N O P Q R S T U V W X Y Z

Written Code
Sheet of Paper

Here are some code messages. Every code used has been explained on pages 108-114. Try each code on the message below until you find the one that works.

Number 1

Here is a message which might have been sent by an American President to a famous American general. Can you read it?

ⱯⳈⲈⲚⲄⴺⴺⱵⱵ, Ɔ.Ⳑ

ⲤⲞⳡ. 22,1942

ⴺⲞⳡ. ⴺⲨⴰⴺⴽⳑⴺ ⱯⳑⳑⱯⴳⴺⴺⴰⲬ:
Ⳑ ⲂⲞⴺⲞⲞ ⟨ⳡⴰ ⴺⳡ ⟨ⲞⳑⴳⲞ ⳙⳑⴺⳑⳑⳑ.
⟨ⳡⴰ ⳑⲂⲞ ⴺⲞⲞⴺⲞⴺ ⳡⳑ ⳑⴰⴺⴺⲞⳑ⟨Ⳑ.
ⴺⳙⲂⲦⲞⴺⳙ ⳙⳡⳑⴺⴺ Ɐⳑ⟨⟨ ⴺⳑⴺⲞ ⟨ⳡⴰ
ⴺⴺⲞⳙⴰⴺⴺ ⴺⴺⲞ ⱯⳑⴿⳑⳑⲞⲈⲞ
ⳙ⟨ⳙⳑⴿⳑⴺⲞ. ⳑ⟨ⳑⳑⲞⲈ Ɐⳑ⟨⟨
ⱯⲞⲞⴺ ⴺⴺⲞ ⳙⳡⳑⴺⴺ. ⴺⳡⳡⴺ
⟨ⳡⳑⳑ⟩.

ⲤⲞⳑⳑⳝ⟨ⳑⳑ Ɔ. ⲐⳡⳡⲈⲞⳡⲞ⟨ⴺ

Number 2

The man whose name is at the bottom of this message did not send it. He was a famous American spy. He did write some letters, but his enemies would not let him send them. Suppose this message did come through. Could you have read it for the famous American general who was to get it?

WALY. 21, 1776

CAJAVEP CAKVCA SEWDMJCYKJ:

CAJAVEP DKSAW IAJ DERA GEQCDY IA. M WDEPP FA DEJCAH EW E WLT YKIKVOKS. M VACVAY YDEY M DERA FQY KJA PMBA YK PKWA BKV IT GKQJYVT.

JEYDEJ DEPA

Number 3

Here is a message which might have come to the White House on December 7, 1941, a date we will long remember.

KBQBOFTF BUUBDLFE QFBSM IBSCPS XJUI GMBOFT BOE TVCNBSJOFT. HSFBC EBNBHF UP PVS TIJQT, QMBOFT BOE GJFMET. NBOZ EFBE. TFOE IFMQ.

Number 4

Here is another message which was never written. But it could have been. Some Americans were cornered in a fort. They needed help badly. They did not get it. If you can read this, you will remember a famous battle in American history.

LQZXKRQN, DQKEI 5, 1836

LTFR ITSH JXOEASN. VT QKT OF ZIT
QSQDG. VT IQCT 180 DTF. LQFZQ QFQ
QFR 4000 DTBOEQF LGSROTKL QKT
GXZLORT. VT IQCT ATHZ ZITD GXZ YGK
ZTF RQNL. EKGEATZZ QFR W GVOT QKT
ITKT WXZ VT EQFFGZ SQLZ DXEI
SGTUTK.

V. W. ZKQCOL

Number 5

During the first World War the American Army
often used pigeons to carry out messages. The Americans in the trenches of the Argonne Forest had over
400 carrier pigeons. The enemy sometimes listened
in on their telephones. They often picked up American radio messages. They might catch a soldier with
a message.

The soldiers put a tiny aluminum message holder
on the pigeon's leg. They wrote the message on thin
paper in code. Here is a code message which might
have been sent by the "Lost Battalion." The Lost
Battalion was surrounded by Germans in the Argonne
Forest. Although badly wounded, their last pigeon
got a coded message through. The Lost Battalion
was saved by a carrier pigeon.

SCHULAR REOLU NEEDILE DOUBELY
GRIEKAR MOASN SUNLE EDDAH EALIP
BREAKED LAYXX

MIALJ OARIC HIAKR LOESS WOHNI
TATIL EMSSIAL EBYXX

Number 6

This is a message which an American general sent by telegraph to the President of the United States. The President had no news of this general and his men for 32 days. Here is the message written in code:

HANNAVASE, AGE.
CEDE. 20, 1864

TNEDISERPE MAHARBAE NLOCNILE:

IE GEBE OTE TNESERPE UOYE SAE AE SAMTSIRHCE TFIGE EHTE YTICE FOE HANNAVASE, HTIWE 150 YVAEHE SNUGE DNAE YTNELPE FOE NOITINUMMAE DNAE OSLAE TUOBAE 25000 SELABE FOE NOTTOCE.

LARENEGE MAILLIWE TE. NAMREHSE

PS
2615
.A1 / 694

CAMROSE LUTHERAN COLLEGE
LIBRARY